Debbie provides you with what you ne
you need to do in order to make the leap into your future.

— Mark LeBlanc, author of *Growing Your Business* and *Never Be The Same*

CLARITY
How Smart Professionals Create
Career Success on Their Terms

Debbie Peterson

Printed in the United States of America

First Printing, 2019

Realtor® is a registered trademark of the National Association of REALTORS®

ISBN 978-1-7336154-0-2

Ordering Information:
Quantity sales. Special discounts are available on quantity purchases by corporations, associations, and others. For details, contact Debbie Peterson of Getting to Clarity, LLC at 814-881-5204, email Debbie@GettingToClarity.com or visit www.GettingTo-Clarity.com.

To my husband, Tom, for helping me to take off the blinders and see my potential, and to my friend, George, for shoving me out of the proverbial nest so I could fly.

CONTENTS

CONTENTS

FOREWORD

By Mark LeBlanc, CSP

In your hands, you hold what could very well be the key to your next level. It might be the next level of your career. It might be the next level of your success. It might be the next level or depth of fulfillment and meaning in your life.

Debbie Peterson is rare indeed and her ability to cut through the noise is astounding. She meets you at the intersection of clarity and truth. Debbie holds up a mirror to what you want in your life and work, whether you want to look into the mirror or not.

What is clear is that reading her book, making decisions, and taking action in the direction of your dream will have profound consequences. It will take a degree of work ethic and work effort to get you where you ultimately want to go. As you move forward, keep this gem at your fingertips and refer to it often.

It can be your desktop or bedside companion and guide you along your way.

Debbie provides you with what you need to know and what you need to do in order to make the leap into your future. At times it will be exciting and at other times you may be nervous or even scared out of your mind.

And that is where life is to be savored and meant to be lived. There has never been a better time to advance in your work and become outstanding in your field.

Make the commitment to answer every question and complete every exercise. You will be glad you did and I guarantee you will never be the same. It is an exciting time and it is your time!

Best.

Mark

PART 1

RESPONSIBILITY

Why You Need to Take Responsibility

"In dreams begin responsibilities."
— W.B. YEATS

T his book starts with a few thoughts on responsibility. I want you to think of responsibility as a privilege, a gift, and most importantly, a key element to building momentum in your business.

When I speak of responsibility, I need to define it. For most people, responsibility is currently a double-edged sword. Right now, you likely are taking responsibility for things that are *none of your business* and a waste of your time and efforts. I want you to focus on three things instead. With your focus on these responsibilities, you will gain more influence and control over your career and create the results you desire.

These are the three pillars of your responsibility at a high level.

1. **What you want.** Do you know what you want next in your career? Many people when forced to ponder that question can't come up with a specific answer. Most people will know that they want to progress, get promoted, be happy or fulfilled, but

aren't able to define what success means to them. If you mean to move forward, then you have to know what you're moving toward; otherwise, you waste your time and efforts.

2. **Why you want it.** It's important to know *why* you want what you want in your career because your *why* is your motivation. It's what keeps you going when things get tough, and if you want to make a leap in your career, that means you're stretching yourself. Things will likely get uncomfortable. Your goals should scare you a little bit. Otherwise, they aren't big enough. Have you thought about *why* you want what you want?

3. **The feedback you get**. Finally, the feedback you get from the actions you take is a gift. Being open to feedback and using it to your advantage is a *mindset shift* the most successful people on the planet understand. The "limit switch" on the acceleration of your career disappears when you understand and embrace feedback. It is a very powerful element of growing, not only professionally, but personally too.

Sheryl Sandberg, COO of Facebook, was asked in an interview, "What's the number one thing you look for in someone who can scale with a company?" and she replied, "feedback." She said, "Because people who can take feedback well are people who can learn and grow quickly."[1]

---

[1] Bariso, Justin. "It Took Sheryl Sandberg Exactly 2 Sentences to Give the Best Career

Are you ready to get clarity on what you're responsible for to grow in your career?

Advice You'll Hear Today." Inc.com. October 31, 2016. Accessed December 10, 2018. https://www.inc.com/justin-bariso/it-took-sheryl-sandberg-exactly-2-sentences-to-give-the-best-career-advice-youll.html.

CHAPTER 1

Something's Got To Give

"If you always do what you've always done,
you'll always get what you've always got."
—Henry Ford

A re you at the "something has to give" stage? There are times when we live in a sea of frustration, and the feelings of being stuck are threatening to pull us under. Yet we often resist making a change in our career because it is tied so closely with our livelihood and we don't want to risk change. We're comfortable with where we are. We are fearful of making a change, but that fear gets the better end of the deal. Fear has more power. Fear gets to run the show. Fear automatically wins the race because we don't even enter it.

I remember one December evening standing at my kitchen window. It was cold, and I was watching fat snowflakes drift lazily to the ground. Tears were streaming down my face because I was so frustrated. I was doing everything I knew (and what everybody told me was right) to grow my business. My frustration had built to the point that it turned to anger, and I actually walked away from it all for a couple of weeks.

That's when I got clarity.

That break allowed me to get *clear* on what I really wanted in my business. It got me clear on what I needed to do. I had more focus afterward because I could see exactly what was going to move me forward according to what I wanted my business to be, not what anyone else's vision was. That was when I knew I could achieve it.

And, believe me, if I can do it, then you can, too. You just need to understand how to go about it, and that's what I'm going to share with you.

You can't achieve significant momentum without clarity. Let's put it this way: you wouldn't just show up at an airport, ponder the departures screen, and then decide where you want to go on vacation that day, right? You would think ahead about destinations, narrow them down, do some research. You would have flights booked; you would have a reservation at a hotel. You would have packed the right clothes for the weather. If you didn't like a particular hotel or destination, you wouldn't go back again; you'd pick something different.

It's the same for your career. You have to start putting thought into what experience you want to have in your professional life. Not just what you're good at or the specific tasks and responsibilities of a job—you also need to understand what you want to experience and feel, so that what you are doing each day leaves you fulfilled instead of frustrated and empty.

Three Reasons Why You Need to Embrace Change In Your Career

- **The first reason** is, *that which you resist persists.* People are uncomfortable making a change. We oppose change for so long that until we are truly miserable, we won't do anything about it. When we feel dissatisfied, unmotivated, or frustrated, those are indicators that we are meant to make a change. It's a sign; it's an inner knowing that we aren't doing what we're supposed to do. We're not doing what makes us tick.

  If what you are doing isn't working and you've given it the good old college try, then it's time for some clarity, especially if what you are doing doesn't make you feel good. Then you know it's time for a change.

  It's not the broad, sweeping changes that will move you forward; it's the small, incremental, specific, consistent ones. Decisions become easier to make. You are more confident about how you will spend your time and money (your two most precious resources). You will be more focused, and most importantly, you will be creating momentum in your career.

- **The second reason** is, it's a *different business environment today* than in the past—one that is more competitive, and on a global scale. To succeed in this environment, you need to be an advocate for yourself and your business. You need to know your value, understand what you bring to the table, and be able to articulate it to your clients and customers.

Today, you have to be able to speak directly to clients, make it easy for them to find you, and be consistent in your messaging and outreach efforts. Do you blog? Vlog? Write articles for industry magazines? Hold webinars? Some of these channels and technologies may be outside of your comfort zone, but that may be exactly where you have to go.

Technology can be a blessing (also a curse at times) that can propel your business to another level. Are you embracing it? Are you continuing to learn what resources will help you stay in front of your customers and clients? Because if you're not speaking to them regularly, someone else is.

- **The third reason** is, the *quick solution you're looking for doesn't exist.* We all want quick fixes. We all want to do one thing that will have a *big* impact but often aren't willing to give it time to allow it to work. If you find yourself trying the *newest* or *next best thing* on a frequent basis, this could be you.

One of the hazards for me early in my business was "Squirrel Syndrome." I saw other entrepreneurs and businesses that seemed to be hitting it out of the park and thought, "Oh, if they are successfully doing that, then I need to do that, too." I was quickly adding more and more to my plate, going in a million different directions, accomplishing exactly nothing. Which, of course, led to more frustration and stress.

Building your business, your client base, your referral network, and other such critical processes doesn't happen overnight. It's not fast, and it's not necessarily easy, but you have to be willing to commit to the time and resources to do it. There are no shortcuts.

You have to be willing to make the change and then stick to it long enough to give it the time to work.

CHAPTER 2

You Can't Hit a Bullseye without a Target

"It's a lack of clarity that creates chaos and frustration."
—STEVE MARABOLI

I can't tell you how many people I meet when I speak, coach, and train who are unable to tell me exactly what they want in their business.

They can tell me what they *don't* want. "I don't want to fail. I don't want to be stuck here." Or if they think they do know what they want, it's still too vague, so it's not attainable. I hear things like, "I need to get more clients," or, "I want to be successful," or, "I need to make more money." And when I ask specifically how *much* more money, they don't have a ready answer. When I ask what their plan is to generate more clients, they develop a proverbial deer-in-the-headlights look.

These people are able to say they want something different, but they aren't able to say exactly what that is; that sort of clarity is important for a number of reasons.

I used to be one of those people, feeling there was something more for me, but having no idea what it was or how to go about finding it. It's a frustrating place to be. The worst part was that I would mentally beat myself up for not being able to figure it out—kind of like when you're having a bad day, and you heap everything that's not going well in your life onto your plate and get really upset about it. We can be our own worst enemies, especially with our mindsets.

The reason that having clarity in business is so important is that your unconscious mind is your biggest advocate for creating influence in your business. It constantly seeks out what you tell it to find, and you do that via the instructions you give it. Those instructions are the words that you use and the thoughts that you think. To give your mind maximum clarity, your instructions must focus on what you want to create in business, and not on what you don't. Anytime you find yourself saying or thinking "I don't want this," your job is to ask, "what do I want instead?" This will continually move you in the direction of your goals.

For example, if you're thinking, "I just don't want to work seventy hours a week anymore," ask yourself instead, "How many hours a week do I want to work?" And answer. The answer becomes part of your goal, and you're now focused on what you want instead of what you don't.

Here's the reason. You've doubtless seen commercials for new cars. And at some point, you've probably thought to yourself, "I like that specific car; it's pretty cool. I wonder how much it costs." Your thoughts are now on that particular car.

You go to the bank and suddenly you notice that car is in the drive-through teller line. Next, you see it in the parking lot when you go to the store. Later you see it in your neighbor's driveway, too! You only watch twenty minutes of television a day, but now you see that commercial six more times. It's like that car is *everywhere*. Now: was the car around the day before? Yes. But it wasn't your focus then. That's the power of your mind. It will focus on and seek out what you want and filter out all the rest.

Back to vacation planning: When you go on vacation, you've typically done some research. You know your destination, what the weather should be like there, and you've packed appropriate clothes. You may have a budget. You may have excursions planned. You may have dinner or show reservations. My point is, you've put time and effort into figuring out what you would enjoy and then set it up.

When was the last time you did that same level of planning for your career? How can you know where you'd like to go in your career if you haven't thought about where that may be?

Here are some questions that can help illuminate what you'd like your career to become. Grab a journal or a tablet and answer each question to the best of your ability. Remember: Always phrase your answers in the direction of what you *do* want, not what you don't.

Career Vision Clarity Questions

1. What specifically do you want your business or career to be? Corporate? A boutique-style business? Local or regional leader? Somewhere in between?

2. What do you want to earn? Do you want to earn a million dollars per year, or is $100,000 a sweet deal for you?

3. How much do you want to work? Per day? Per week? Per month?

4. How much flexibility do you need?

5. Where do you want to work from? Home? Office? Co-work space? On the road?

6. Do you want to be able to travel while you work?

7. Do you want to be a solopreneur or build a team?

8. Do you want to work for an organization or with an organization as a partner?

9. What types of clients or customers do you specifically want to work with?

10. How much time do you want available to do other things, like spending time with family, working out, or volunteering to do things that are important to you?

11. What is your absolute most favorite thing to do in your career? What will it look like if you do more of it?

You also need to know that going after what you want in business is a *process*, not a project. You may start in one place and end up in another, and that's OK. It takes time and trial-and-error to figure out what most fulfills us. Even as adults, most of us are still trying to figure out what we want to be when we grow up.

When I started my business, it was as a life coach, and although I enjoyed it, it didn't really feel like it was my thing. Then one day I got up in front of an audience of 300 with a microphone and delivered my first speech. I didn't pass out, so that was an indicator that I was onto something! I shared tips and strategies as well as stories and examples from my life. I made a connection with so many people in the audience that day, and they knew they weren't the only ones to feel like they do. More importantly, they knew they didn't have to figure it out by themselves.

My business took a turn that day, and it's taken other turns since then, but my point is that you have to pick a lane. You have to have a focus regarding what you want your business to be and then take action on it. Only then will you know what turns may be ahead for you. Nothing ventured, nothing gained.

CHAPTER 3

What's Your Why?

"If it's important to you, you'll find a way.
If not, you'll find an excuse."
—UNKNOWN

D o you know your *why*? Many people conflate this
question with finding a purpose—their spiritual
understanding of whom they are meant to be. It's
an important element in the business setting as well as a
critical element for professionals who want more influence over their business.

Knowing your *why* is a crucial piece of your success
in business. It is the reason you want to do what you're
doing in the first place. When you're starting a business
or taking it to the next level, the *why* is critical. You really
have to know why you want to make a move. Your *why* is
going to keep you company through this journey and will
keep you moving when you feel like quitting. You can't
do what you want to do without it.

My daughter-in-law just graduated with a doctor-
ate in physical therapy, and there are many directions in
which she could go with that degree: physical therapy of-
fices, sports practices, pediatric concentrations, hospital
settings, and more. She chose to pursue the in-hospital

setting because she really wants to make a big difference in the quality of life for people who have had a debilitating illness or accident. That is her *why*.

Knowing your *why* speaks to your motivation. There will be plenty of days when things won't go right. Your *why* will get you out of bed, keep you taking steps forward and moving toward your business goals when you really don't feel like it.

Your *why* will also help you deal with sacrifices. Pursuing the next BIG move for your business can require sacrifice: for example, business development isn't a quick process. You have to be visible, continually reach out to prospects, build relationships. All of that takes time. It can mean a lot of hours. Being consistent can also mean time away from family and friends. It can mean that you are up early, out late, giving up your weekends for open houses or your nights for committee meetings and other social events that build your visibility and credibility in the community. It can mean that you are in your car...a lot. But that's what it takes to arrive at the level that you aspire to. When you know your *why*, it makes sacrifice more palatable.

When I started my business, it was a big shift into the entrepreneurial world. I walked away from the 8:00–5:00 job, steady paycheck, great benefits, and nights, weekends, and holidays off. Today, I work from the house, which gives me a great deal of flexibility, but the days, nights, weekends, and even holidays can blend together with my business.

I used to love to fish with my husband, and it's been at least a year since I've gone, but I know it takes time and effort to take a business to the next level. Now I travel more to speak and train people in the system contained in this book. It has transformed my career and business, and now I want to pay that forward so others can experience it, too. That's my *why*. I love doing it, and it's meaningful to me and to the people I serve.

But what if you don't have a clue what your *why* is? Sometimes when you don't know your *why*, it's trial and error to figure it out. For my daughter-in-law, the decision to pursue in-hospital physical therapy came when she was in school and had a chance to try other specialties in her rotations. She worked with pediatrics in a school district and spent another rotation in a hospital. That's when she found out what lit her up.

For me, I had to try different ways of being of service to people. I stumbled on speaking by accident but knew right away it was going to be a big part of my business. It tied into my *why* because it allowed me to serve a bigger audience. Speaking lights me up.

Let's talk a moment about what your *why* isn't.

If your *why* is "a good paycheck," that's not enough. Money is not a long-term motivator. If you're miserable in your business, no amount of money is going to make you happy. You may have convinced yourself that it is the reason to keep going, but it certainly won't make you any happier.

Your *why* needs to be personal. That may sound redundant, but people have taken on running businesses because that was what expected of them. It's what their family has always done (Mom is a banker, Dad is a financial planner, etc.). I call that a *hand-me-down why*. It's not yours. It belongs to someone else. At its core, your *why* is personal to you. It's emotional. It means something to you, and you feel it.

Let's consider your business: Why do you do it? Are you having success? Do you have a chance to make an impact in your industry or maybe the world? When you understand what lights you up, you have a chance to make choices that move you toward *more* of that. You get clarity on how you spend your time and your money— your two most precious resources.

What Are Ways You Can Find Your *Why?*

Write down every reason why you are doing what you are doing. When you get an answer, drill down again and ask, "Why is that?" Eventually, you will get to the essence of your true *why*. Pay attention to it and look at ways to incorporate tasks and responsibilities that fit with your *why*.

You can also speak to friends, coworkers or family members. Ask them what you're good at or what makes you a really great real estate agent, financial planner, banker, etc. What is easy for you to do that isn't so easy for others? If you identify a pattern, that can be a good indicator of your *why*, or lead you to it.

Your *Why* Clarity Questions

1. Why do you do what you do?

2. What does it allow you to be?

3. What does it allow you to do?

4. What does it allow you to have?

5. What would happen if you didn't?

6. Why is it important to you?

CHAPTER 4

Which Are You Getting?
Reasons or Results?

"Thought is cause: Experience is effect. If you don't like the effects in your life, you have to change the nature of your thinking."
—MARIANNE WILLIAMSON

W hen you are fully responsible for getting the results you want in your business, you are learning something from each and every action you take. You are able to glean valuable feedback and make necessary adjustments so that you are continually moving toward your business goals. When you are able to continually move forward, you have found a way to create more influence over what happens in your business. In other words, you're making it happen.

If, however, you have a litany of *reasons* why you cannot achieve your career goals, then you've surrendered any power, control, or influence over those reasons.

- **"I can't start a business because I don't have enough experience."** I guess no one told Richard Branson, Arianna Huffington, Walt Disney, or Rachel Ray. They didn't have experience, either.

Richard Branson had no formal higher education and no business training. He just started doing what he enjoyed, and his business grew from there. If you hold onto the excuse, then it defines you.

- **"I'm too old to think about starting a business."** Martha Stewart started her magazine at the age of fifty, and Colonel Harlan Sanders was sixty-five when he started the chain of Kentucky Fried Chicken franchises. I guess they didn't get the memo about age.

- **"I don't have the confidence to get ahead."** What steps are you taking to get it? Are you exposing yourself to manageable risk so that you can accomplish things that will build confidence? Have you taken any steps to address any self-worth issues you may have?

- **"I don't have the connections necessary to build my business."** OK, you may not *now*, but what are you doing to change that? Are you attending industry or social functions? Are you being visible by participating on committees? Are you networking? Are you volunteering?

- **"I don't have any idea what I need to do to get ahead in my business."** If that's truly the case, go back to chapter 2 and start answering your Business Vision Clarity Questions. Then find the resources that are going to help you get where you need to go. Take a course, read a book, or hire a coach. Meet with people who interest you and are doing what you want. Ask them what they did, what they enjoy, and see if it gives you direction.

- **"I don't know how to start a business."** Neither did I, but that didn't stop me. There are many resources out there to help, like the SBA (Small Business Administration) and its local chapter SBDC (Small Business Development Corporation). You also have access to more books, courses, webinars, online resources, and coaches than you can shake a stick at, if a business is what you want to create.

When you point your finger at a reason, a person, or a circumstance that you believe limits you or holds you back from going for what you want, I want you to pay attention. Self-awareness is key to making any sort of change. So, when you "point your finger" at a specific reason why you can't be, do, or have what you want in your business, where are the remaining three fingers pointed?

Yes, that would be at *you*. That's where the responsibility lies; with you, not with anyone or anything else. If you want it, then you're the one who has to go get it. Every time you are not getting the result that you want, look at the reasons why. Are you going to let those reasons stop you? It's OK to not know all the answers, but it is *not* OK to not work at figuring them out.

My point is that you are either limited or flexible in your mindset when it comes to what you want. You either know that you can learn it or figure it out, or you think you no longer have the ability to influence the situation or outcome.

Are you are making your business happen, or you are allowing it to *happen to you*? That's a key concept.

There a number of ways that you become responsible for your results; we're going to cover those that will most directly impact your influence in business. They are:

- Your values around business

- Mistakes

- Boundaries

- Being the straw

- Lessons

CHAPTER 5

What Do You Value?

---

*"It's not hard to make decisions once you
know what your values are."*

—Roy E. Disney

D o you know what is most valuable to you in creating and running your business? Do you know what needs to be present for you to be fulfilled in business? Do you know how you want to experience your business? If not, how to do you expect to get it?

It's not just the tasks and responsibilities of running your business that you need to consider when making decisions; it's your business values. Let me give you an example.

A task is *reaching out to prospective clients*. A value is *enjoyment*, which would include *how* you go about reaching out to clients. However you perform tasks in your business, you should find a way to do them in ways you enjoy.

If you aren't sure what your values are for your business, you can end up in situations that are a bad fit, or, worse yet, in situations that undermine your self-esteem and erode your confidence and influence.

Values are what are most important to you. In the context of business, values are what need to be present for you to be *fulfilled* in your business. What must you experience? What is a deal-breaker? Values are most important to you in business as an *individual*. They are personal—not what you think you *should* value, or what someone else says is important. It's all about you.

Values determine how you spend your time, and also how you value the time you have spent doing things in your business. Think about the last time you uttered the phrase, "Well, that was a complete waste of time." Whatever it was that you had just completed did not align with your values, and therefore you were disappointed.

Your values around business are typically unconscious until you bring them to light, which is what we are about to do. When you have explored and understand your own values related to business, you can more easily make decisions that will bring you happiness and protect your overall satisfaction.

I want to give you an example, but I'm not going to use business. I'm going to use another area of life instead: relationships. The reason is I don't want to "seed" a value in your mind when you do this exercise for your business; it needs to be 100 percent yours.

If I'm looking to get into a romantic relationship, to help clarify my values, I would ask myself, "What is most important *to be present* in a relationship?" I'm looking for one- or two-word descriptors. I might say things like *pas-*

sion, love, respect, consideration, or *understanding.* These are things I want to experience in a relationship. I would go with the words that pop into my mind right away. I would keep asking myself that question until I have come up with a good list of one- or two-word answers.

Clarity Exercise for Eliciting Values

1. Ask yourself, "What is most important to me in the context of career?" Relate the question to an area of life such as Career, Relationships, Health and Fitness, Spirituality, Personal Development or Family. Ask and answer this question again and again until you absolutely can't think of anything else. Leave it for a period of time and come back to it in case something else comes to you.

2. So now you've got a list going (at least ten answers). As you look at the list, ask yourself, "If all of this on my list is present, is there anything that could cause me to leave, stop, quit, etc.?" Identify that, give it a name, and then flip it to the positive and make sure that is on your list too. So, for example, if in the context of Career, someone at work like your supervisor would *disrespect* you and that's a deal-breaker, then make sure whatever the opposite for you is (perhaps *respect* is the term you would use) is on the list.

3. Now that you have a comprehensive list, you need to *prioritize* it. It's not looking at the list and saying "Ok, this is number 1, this is number 2,

and this is number 3." Instead, consider one item at a time and compare it to each other item on your list.

Look at the first item on your list. Is it more important than the second item? Then it ranks number 1 (for now). Next, compare number 1 to the third item on your list. If it's still number 1, then move on to the fourth item. If, while comparing, another item takes over the number one spot, there is no need to go back. This is now the most important item; you'll eventually compare it to the rest of your list.

Now, look at the first item *remaining* on your list that isn't assigned a place or number and use the same procedure as above, comparing it to every item remaining on the list to arrive at your second priority. Continue this way for every item in order to rank and arrive at your true priorities.

The following tool may help you as you go through this values clarification exercise.

Questions to Elicit and Rank Values

Step 1: Answer Questions to Create a List of Values

What is most *important* to you in the context of career? What *must* be present?

Can you remember a specific time when you were totally motivated in the context of career?

As you remember that time, what was the last thing you felt just before you were totally motivated? What was important to you about that?

You are looking for one- or two-word answers, not sentences.

STEP 1: List Values   **STEP 2: Prioritize**

1. _____   _____

2. _____   _____

3. _____   _____

4. _____   _____

5. _____   _____

6. _____   _____

7. _____   _____

8. _____   _____

9. _____   _____

10. _____   _____

If all of this were present, is there anything that would have to happen to make you stop/quit/leave? Is there a deal-breaker? What is the positive opposite of this? Add this to your list if it isn't already there.

Step 2: Prioritize values according to their value to you by assigning a number to each. Compare a single value to every other value on the list before moving on to prioritize the next value.

While going through your list, you may find that some words actually mean the same thing to you (for example *respect* and *courtesy* may mean the same thing). Keep whichever word you feel the most strongly about.

When you get into a situation in which you are torn and believe that two items on your list are equally as important, you still need to choose one. So, try this: Ask yourself, "If I could *always* have _____ but *never* have _____, is that better than the opposite?" Then flip them and select. For instance, in the context of Career, if I could always have *passion (for what I do)* but never have *respect*, is that better than always having *respect* but never having *passion*? Sometimes forcing a choice makes you really think about what is most important; that is the goal of this exercise.

When you are all finished with your list, be proud of the scribbles, cross-outs, and rewrites—they mean you're doing your internal work.

Now rewrite your list in order of importance and keep it handy. Add to this list and change it as your circumstances change. It might stay the same; it might not. But whatever happens, it's perfect for you.

Here's a sample of what the exercise would look like.

Sample: Completed Values Clarity Exercise

What's important to me in the context of business?

1. Passion
2. Compensated fairly
3. Learning and growing
4. Serving others
5. Travel
6. Speaking opportunities
7. Teaching
8. Fun
9. Work from home
10. Flexibility
11. Collaboration

If all of this is present in my business, is there anything that could happen that would cause me to leave, quit or stop?

Yes, disrespect.

Ok, what is the opposite of disrespect to me?

Respect.

1. *Passion*
2. *Compensated fairly*
3. *Learning and growing*
4. *Serving others*
5. *Travel*
6. *Speaking opportunities*
7. *Teaching*
8. *Fun*
9. *Work from home*
10. *Flexibility*
11. *Collaboration*
12. *Respect*

Ok, now it's time to prioritize:

- Is *Passion* more important in the context of business or *Compensated fairly*? Hmmmm. Those are both pretty important. If I could always have *Pas-*

sion but never be *Compensated fairly* OR always be *Compensated fairly* but never have *Passion*, which would I pick? *Passion*. So, *Passion* is my #1.

- Now I compare *Passion* to *Learning and growing*. *Passion* is still #1.

- *Passion* compared to *Serving others*? *Passion* is still #1

- *Passion* compared to *Travel*, and so on.

- Now take *Compensated fairly* because it is next on the list and compare it to each item remaining on the list. No need to compare it to *Passion*, because we already know that's #1. So *Compensated fairly* compared to *Learning and growing*. For me, it's *Learning and growing*.

- So now I take *Learning and growing* and continue to the next item because I've already determined it's more important than *Compensated fairly*. *Learning and growing* or *Serving others*, etc.

Here is what my list ended up looking like:

1. Passion
2. Learning and growing
3. Serving others
4. Respect
5. Compensated fairly
6. Travel
7. Fun
8. Flexibility
9. Collaboration

Notice the list shrunk? In this example, *Teaching* is how I am going to *Serve others,* so they were synonymous. Also, *Flexibility* meant the same as *Working from home.*

Values are a big deal. They are what will allow you to achieve what you want. When they are in alignment with your work, they will feed your motivation and pull you toward your career goals. When they aren't, they will stop you in your tracks. You choose.

CHAPTER 6

Mistakes

"Anyone who has never made a mistake
has never tried anything new."
—ALBERT EINSTEIN

Have you ever made a mistake? An *OMG I can't believe I did that!* kind of mistake? A *What was I thinking!* kind of mistake?

Have you ever reacted poorly to a person, situation, or circumstance in your business environment? Do you beat yourself up afterward? Feel guilty? How about a hefty dose of regret, followed by continual rumination on your major blunder?

What good does that do?

Actually, plenty. It's a sign that you need to take action.

Whatever has been done is done. It is water under the bridge, and when it comes to having more influence in building your business, the only thing you have control over is your *reaction*. Do you need to make amends? Is there someone you offended to whom you need to apologize? Admitting that you were wrong can be one of the hardest things to do, but it is also when you own up to and take responsibility for your mistakes that you build credibility. The key is that by taking responsibility for a mistake, you are also learning a lesson and taking different action as a result.

When I moved to Florida, I was also just starting my business. I was looking to make contacts in my new community to establish and grow my business. One name kept coming up again and again with people I'd meet. They'd say, "You need to meet Christin." Christin, as it turns out, is one of the most connected people in my area; I made it my mission to get a meeting with her and did.

On the day of the meeting, however, I stood her up. She was a key person who could make many introductions for me and my business, and I blew her off, all because the meeting with her went into my phone at the wrong time. I needed to take responsibility for my mistake, and so I called and explained what had happened. I wasn't making excuses. I owned up to my error, apologized, and asked for another meeting.

Here's the point of this story. Do you think the next time I went to put a meeting into my phone, I double-checked to make sure it went in at the right time? *You bet I did.*

You have to learn something from your mistakes *and* take different action as a result.

There will be situations that turn out unfavorably, and the biggest tip I can give you is you've got to learn as much from them as you can. Why? Because it helps you to learn about yourself, your values, what is acceptable and what is not, and most importantly, what to do differently the next time. It allows you to make progress.

Here's what else you need to know about your new-found friend, the mistake.

- **A mistake is merely a choice that doesn't serve you well.** While listening to a recording of a webinar one day, I heard that, and it stuck with me. I loved it because the use of the word *choice* says that you have other options. You can make *another choice* and realize a *different outcome*. Mistakes aren't necessarily bad; they allow you to grow. I know you've said at some point, "Well, I'll never do that again." Same deal: Make a different choice the next time and know you've learned a valuable lesson from your mistake.

- **There is no failure, only feedback.** *If* what happens as a result of a decision or action is not what you want, then incorporate the feedback or lesson from it and do it differently the next time. You take different action as a result of the feedback. Say, for instance, you are driving to an appointment in the morning. You've cut it close on timing and suddenly come upon a construction detour. You know you won't make it on time; the traffic is snarled, and you're worried about making this important meeting. If the next day you choose another route or leave a little earlier, then congratulations; you've incorporated the feedback. It's as simple as that. You have opportunities to learn from less-than-favorable circumstances.

- **Don't give away your personal power.** When you say that things *"happen to you,"* or anytime you believe you are the *"victim"* in a situation or whatever happened was an *"accident,"* you have just given away any opportunity you could seize to make a difference for yourself. You have *said* that person, that situation is more important, more powerful, and more in control than you. You just gave away your personal power. Instead, look at the situation with an eye for how *you* could influence the circumstances the next time, no matter how subtly.

  One little change means it's not happening the *same* way the next time, and that's progress. Every time you say "No" to something you don't want to do, you have learned from an experience. Every time you declare that someone or something is unacceptable to you because you deserve more— and you act on it—you have learned from an experience. Every time you refuse to get swirled into someone else's drama—because they live for drama—you have learned from an experience.

- **Ditch the (negative) emotion.** When you make a mistake, often you come down hard on yourself. You beat yourself up. You dwell on it. You wake up in the middle of the night and obsess about it. You then wake up in the morning, after finally having fallen asleep and forgotten your huge and perceived tragic misdeed, only to remember seconds after opening your eyes what happened... and it's downhill again. What you are feeling is being felt for a reason. Feelings are meant to inspire us to action. Picture a fearful caveman facing a hungry, drooling tiger: He's meant to take action—to run—so he doesn't become lunch. Your feelings are telling you to take action as well. Do you need to make amends? Do you need to create a new plan? Do you need to do something different as a result of what happened? Whatever it is, your feelings around this issue are meant for you to do something *different* as a result. Then you're meant to let the emotion go. It no longer serves a purpose if you've taken appropriate action. But what frequently happens is that we hold it close, continue to focus on it, and it distorts our way forward. Ditch the emotion, learn your lesson, and take different action the next time. You'll have much more *clarity* when you can look at something without emotion.

As you start recognizing the impact you can have on your business just by learning from your experiences, it gets easier. Notice when you have little *Aha!* moments— those are your learnings at work. Be grateful for them. Journal them so you can see the progress you are making.

Knowing that you are only in charge of your role in any situation, and that you have the power to act on it, will allow you to make different decisions that move you forward confidently.

CHAPTER 7

Boundaries: Are People Crossing the Line?

"You get what you tolerate."

—Henry Cloud

D o you remember the game Red Rover from when you were a kid? Two lines of kids face each other, clutched hand-in-hand, shouting "Red Rover, Red Rover, let Cindy come over!" And then Cindy would run from the other side, barreling like a miniature missile, running as fast as her little legs would carry her to try and break through the line. I loved that game, even though I'd hear myself saying "Don't pick Debbie, don't pick Debbie," chanting it again and again in my mind because I was scared to charge the line.

When I think of boundaries, this childhood game pops into my mind. In the game, someone is always trying their best to break through your line. As an adult, it's the same thing with your boundaries, except you may or may not see them coming or be aware of your boundaries being crossed.

Personal boundaries are like a fenced-in yard. The fence is in place to keep some things out and other things in. Boundaries in your professional life are the same.

When someone says something to you, and it doesn't sit well, you have a *feeling* about it. That feeling is an indicator that a boundary has likely been crossed. When someone treats you rudely, and you get angry or irritated, that is a sign that one of your boundaries has been crossed. That feeling means that you are supposed to *do something about it* because it is not acceptable to you.

Here's the thing, though; if you feel that you are being disrespected by someone, you know it's wrong because you have that feeling or are irritated, *and* you do nothing about it, then you have just disrespected yourself. That's right, if you allow your boundaries to be continually crossed and take no action to enforce them, *you are the one being disrespectful.* And it's to *you.* Allowing this to happen repeatedly will kill your confidence and any chance of having influence in the business you desire.

In some cases, it's pretty obvious that your boundaries are being crossed. Say, for instance, someone in your circle is blatantly rude and obnoxious. That might be an easy one; you'll know that you don't care to be around the person, and you'll make changes accordingly to limit or end your time with the person because such behavior is unacceptable to you.

How about when a competitor goes after one of your existing clients? Or you hear through the grapevine that a colleague isn't supporting you? How about the team member who always wants something from you, or for you to always help out, but that never comes back to help you when you need it?

Back when I was in the corporate world and very early in my career, I had a supervisor who was very rude to me. I'm a pretty chipper person, and I would walk into the department and say good morning and get no response. The first time, I thought she must not have heard me. The next time it happened, I wondered what I had done to offend her. The third time it happened, I knew this was a boundary violation I couldn't live with and that I had to do something about it. I had to have a very difficult conversation with her, as much as I didn't want to. That was the best thing I could have done, but it wouldn't have happened without my taking the initiative, even though she was the supervisor.

Now, boundaries don't have to be enforced with a sledgehammer. As a matter of fact, the less emotion employed when enforcing your boundaries, the better. In the case of my supervisor, I asked if she had time to speak for a moment in an empty office. I explained to her what was happening, how it made me feel, and asked if we could find a resolution. We agreed on professionalism. We didn't have to be best friends, but we now had a good professional relationship that was respectful.

I'm not going to say it was easy to enforce that particular boundary. She was my supervisor, and I felt like I wanted to lose my breakfast when I asked to speak to her, but it was necessary.

Top 10 Signs You Need Healthy Boundaries

1. You're last in line. Everyone seems to come before you when it comes to your time.

2. At one point, you enjoyed doing favors, but now you feel you "have to."

3. You feel *guilty* if you don't.

4. You keep *hoping* something will change, but it never does.

5. You take too much on and won't ask for help.

6. No one else wants to do it. So now you feel you *have to*.

7. You feel resentment.

8. You constantly feel overwhelmed.

9. As much as you help others, there is never anyone to help you when you need it.

10. You say you're going to stop it, but that never seems to happen.

Boundary Clarity Exercise

1. Write down **three** people whom you feel intentionally or *unintentionally* cross your boundaries. They take up too much of your time or generally are energy vampires (for those of you who aren't familiar with the term, they suck the life out of you).

2. Write down **one** event or circumstance that you'd be happy to not spend your precious time on. It's

not that it's unworthy; it's just not how you would choose to spend your time.

3. If you didn't have to worry about how you'd be perceived or someone's feelings didn't factor into your decision, write down **one** choice you'd make instead.

4. What is **one** step you can take to move you in the direction of what you want? Just one little step? Do it today.

CHAPTER 8

Be the Straw

"Rule your mind or it will rule you."

—HORACE

One of my favorite demonstrations when I speak to audiences is to hand out straws. The audience members invariably kind of look at me funny and wonder what they are supposed to do with them, but when I explain the purpose of the straws, it's life-changing.

What I'd like you to do right now is to go to your kitchen or breakroom and get a straw if one is available. Once you have it, I want you to tell me, "What is the job of the straw?" If you were writing a job description for a straw, what would its responsibilities be?

Instead of making you do that, I'll tell you: The job of the straw is to convey liquid from the receptacle you are drinking out of so the liquid passes through it and into your mouth so you can swallow it. It can also be used to launch spitballs, but since this book is written for professionals, I would hope those days are gone.

What happens when you are finished drinking? If you pull the straw out of your cup and peer into the end of it, is there any liquid left in it? Perhaps there's a drop or two, but essentially, the straw is empty. It's done its job, and it is now clear, right?

I want you to be the straw.

Every time some cranky individual is doing his or her level best to ruin your day so that you'll be as miserable as them, *be the straw* and let it pass on through. It's not your job to take on somebody else's attitude. It's not your job to be upset about what that person is upset about. You've got enough on your plate, right? You really don't need to add anyone else's baggage to your day. It's not your job to fix anyone else or their day. It's your job to focus on you and your business. Besides, emotions and attitudes come from within. They are personal. The cranky coworker is the only one who can do anything about his attitude. It's his choice, not your worry. Be the straw.

When It Pays to "Be the Straw"

- **With Drama Queens and Kings:** Some people thrive on drama and the vortex of chaos they love to exist in. I know you know who I mean. Someone popped into your head when I said this. Don't get sucked into their drama; that chaos doesn't belong to you unless you make the decision to let it affect you. This used to be me. I used to say that *I was good in chaos* until I realized all I was finding were situations that were chaotic that I had to fix. Once I learned to become the straw, my world got much easier, and I had lots of time to focus on things that benefited me, like my business and how I could create the kind of influence I desired.

- **When someone has an issue with a decision you have made.** It's just that—somebody else's issue. Let the emotion or attitude pass right through. When you do that, you can see the situation through a lens that's clear of emotion.

- **With people who don't like you.** This was a tough one for me. How could people not like me? I'm nice, I'm friendly, *I don't understand.* Trust me, there will be people who don't like you or will have an issue with you. *What other people think of you is none of your business.* It is their opinion, it's their attitude, it's their responsibility. Not yours.

- **With gossipers.** I've always had the attitude that if someone's gossiping about me, then I should be flattered. Obviously, I'm doing something that warrants their time and attention. When someone gossips about someone else, they are trying to elevate themselves by putting someone else down. They are using someone else to make themselves appear better in some way. It's cruel and it's unnecessary, and it's also a big credibility robber when it comes to influence in your professional life. Do not participate in gossip; walk away instead, because even if you are in a group and not saying a thing, you are *still participating* in gossip.

CHAPTER 9

Lessons: Learn the Lesson Before the Two-by-Four

"The past is where you learned the lesson.
The future is where you apply it."

—UNKNOWN

B ack in chapter 4, we talked about having reasons why you may not be achieving your desired results, or you are achieving results because you are incorporating your lessons or learnings.

Lessons are feedback. Lessons are the pearls of wisdom we get from each situation or circumstance that we encounter. For instance, in chapter 6 when I spoke of my disastrous nonmeeting with Christin, my lesson was to double-check what time I put in my phone for meetings. That was my feedback and what I needed to adjust to get a different result.

Lessons can be big or small, but you definitely want to learn them *sooner than later.* Lessons are from your unconscious. Almost all of your thinking is done at an unconscious level, so if you want to make change in your professional life, it won't happen until you change—specifically, until you change your mindset.[2]

---

[2] Szegedy-Maszak, Marianne. "Mysteries of the Mind Your Unconscious Is Making Your Everyday Decisions." *US News & World Report.* Last modified February 28, 2005.

In the world of mindset change, your conscious mind is the goal-setter, but your unconscious mind is the goal-getter. Your unconscious mind works tirelessly to bring you information that will help you improve and move closer toward your goals, but you have to pay attention to reap the rewards.

You also must know that lessons are repeated until we get them, and the bigger they get, the more uncomfortable they can become.

What happens many times is people don't want to absorb the lesson. They don't want to "deal" with it. They'd rather "power through" the situation, keep moving forward, than learn their lessons.

Lessons by nature have to get larger each time you repeat them. If you didn't get it the first time around, it must not have been important enough for you to make a change, so it will be bigger the next time and bigger the next time still. Finally, here comes the BIG two-by-four to smack you right between the eyes. It's much easier, however, to listen to the subtle messages of your intuition than to be laid low by the two-by-four.

Your new go-to question needs to be, "What can I learn from this?" In every situation that seems unfavorable to you, don't take it personally; ask this question instead and get the pearl of wisdom that will allow you to continue to grow and evolve professionally.

Here's an example of what I mean from my own professional life.

---

https://web.archive.org/web/20050224091139/http://www.usnews.com/usnews/health/articles/050228/28think.htm.

Back in my corporate days, I worked at a company where we hired a new CEO. He was an outgoing, energetic former sales executive who had had a very successful career (and the ego to go with it). Long story short, he wasn't a good fit. He and the chairman, who was also the founder and owner of the company, didn't gel and things started going downhill fast.

The more results declined at the company, the more the mood and attitude of this CEO changed—negatively. He'd yell, swear, slam doors. Everyone was walking on eggshells. Especially me, as I sat right next door.

It was such an uncomfortable environment, I remember thinking, *if only I could work from home and not have to deal with this on a daily basis; I don't want to be here.*

Well, it didn't improve, and as a matter of fact, it got worse. It was so awful going to work that as I would pull into the parking lot each day and glance at the building, I would feel this kinesthetic feeling of just...*Ugh*. A heaviness. A feeling of dread.

OK, so let me ask you right here, before I tell you what happened: If I am thinking, "I don't want to be here," do you think I'm getting some sort of feedback about how this situation is affecting me? Yes.

Did I listen? No.

What happened next was that I got the two-by-four. I wasn't paying attention to how my work environment was affecting me. I sprained a rib. Did you know that you can sprain a rib? Well let me tell you, it's painful. So, for the next five weeks, I was working from home (isn't that what I wanted?), on muscle relaxers and painkillers, going to the physical therapist, massage therapist, and chiropractor.

Be careful what you wish for because your mind will find a way to make it happen.

What you hear yourself saying is feedback. Your experiences as a result of the action you take are feedback. What you feel as a result of any situation, work or otherwise, is feedback. This internal guidance system is built just for you. Use it. Pay attention and don't doubt what it says because it has your best interest at heart and you shouldn't have to experience the two-by-four as I did to get it.

PART 2

ACCOUNTABILITY

Why You Need Accountability

---

*"Accountability is the glue that ties
commitment to results."*

—BOB PROCTOR

T o make actionable progress on any professional
goal and increase your influence on how you experience your professional life, you've got to have
accountability. You've got to have a plan, goal, or strategy
that you can follow, and check back with frequently to see
if you're going in the right direction.

When you have accountability to yourself, you are
working your plan, making it a priority, and seeing results. When you have a plan, you know what resources
you have at your disposal, what potential obstacles you
may encounter, and how to deal with them. You know
how to spend your time.

When you have accountability, you are truly in charge
of your results.

"You Gots to Have a Plan"

My sister told me a story of a coworker who was taking her daughter to college in Louisiana. It was post-Hur-
ricane Katrina, and this particular area of the country
was forecasted to encounter another hurricane. While
at the admissions counter, the mother confided her ner-

vousness about the impending weather. The admissions clerk responded to let her know that the school had plans in place that ensured the safety of the students. She finished by saying, "You always gots to have a plan," in her sweet Southern accent.

I thought that was a perfect quote. You do need a plan, and you need a plan to move you toward your goals, creating more influence over the professional life that you want.

When you are following a plan, you know that you are moving toward what you want. It's broken down into steps that are actionable, not overwhelming. You have greater clarity about what you should be doing consistently to get the results that you want. You can see the progress you are making. You can make course corrections when you aren't experiencing what you want.

Goals or plans need to be comprehensive. Many people think that if they write something on an index card and look at it daily, that can be considered a goal. It certainly helps with focus and can be considered a *summary* of a goal, but first, you need to have the details behind it.

Goals should be formulated in paragraphs or pages. When you have finished writing out your goal, you should be able to hand it to strangers, and they'd be able to tell what it is that you want to achieve and how you're going to do it.

What Accountability Is

CHAPTER 10

Make It SMART

---

*"Never give up on something you can't go
a day without thinking about."*

—Unknown

'm a fan of the SMART goal. You may or may not have
heard this term, but for me, it is a process for clarity in
goal setting.

SMART is an acronym for the process of setting up a
well-formed goal. Let's think about a goal that you want
to achieve in your career. What specifically do you want?
We covered this in chapter 2, so let's get as clear as you
can with your goal.

Let's say you want to achieve a certification in your
industry; for the sake of this exercise, it's a CFP (Certified
Financial Planner) certification, which is very specific.

- **S is for *Specific.*** We covered this in chapter 2.
  Your goals need to be specific because you are
  giving instructions to your unconscious mind regarding what you want. Remember, the conscious
  mind is the goal *setter*, but the unconscious mind

is the goal *getter*. Saying that you want to be certified isn't specific. Saying that you want to achieve a Certified Financial Planner designation is very specific, and that's what you're after. You always want to be as specific as you can be.

- **M is for *Measurable*.** Your goals need to be measurable so you can gauge your progress. Especially for bigger goals, it can take a longer period to complete them, and you need to know that you are moving in the right direction. Let's go back to the CFP example. Asking for your boss's approval, signing up for the pre-exam study course, registering for the exam, and receiving your certificate are all steps along the way for the certification. It's a timeline of your progress. What are the measurable increments toward your goal? What key indicators will demonstrate you are making progress toward what you want?

- **A is for *As if now*.** Whenever you are writing a goal, write it in the present tense, as if it is already happening right now. For the CFP example, you would say "It is December 31, 2019, and I *have* achieved my Certified Financial Planner certificate," not "I *will* achieve my Certified Financial Planner certificate." This process is all about your mindset, so you want to give very specific instructions about what happens and when. If you say "I have," your unconscious mind notices and says, *I need to get going*. If you say, "I will have," it thinks *I've still got time* and can go after this later. Phrasing goals in the present tense also gets you used to operating as if the successful outcome has already occurred.

- **R is for *Realistic*.** I'm a fan of the BIG goal, and you want to make sure that your goal is realistic for you or realistic within the timeframe you want it. Your goal may be to become partner in your firm (which could be achievable for you), but if your timeline is one year and you're a first year employee, that's an unrealistic timeline. Your goal may be to earn $150,000 this year, but if in the past five years all you have earned is $45,000, that might be a stretch. Take very large goals and break them into smaller ones and work toward them incrementally to keep them realistic. You want to set yourself up for success and keep yourself motivated.

- **T is for *Timed*.** You always want to attach a date to your goal by which you want to achieve it. You have a much better perspective of what you need to do, when, and how often when the goal is timed. A date puts parameters around the goal. I always start my goals with the phrase, "It is now (insert date)..." You also want to insert a specific date or known calendar event, like December 31, 2019, or the end of the second quarter, or a particular birthday. You are shooting for specific dates because "one day" and "someday" never come. "One day I would like to become a partner at my firm" doesn't cut it.

Break It Down to Make It Easy

So now you have a goal. You've pulled all kinds of glorious information out of your head, and you've made it SMART. Now what do you do?

At this point, the steps in your goal are probably still big. You have to break down your goal into actionable steps to create consistent behavior that will produce the outcome you desire.

For example, if your goal is to achieve CFP certification, one of the steps in your goal would be to study for the exam. You'll want to break that down even further to create a healthy habit: "Study ninety minutes every weekday and meet with my study group once per week."

Take each of the steps in your goal, determine what you have to do to achieve that step, and then keep breaking it down until you have a set of specific actions you are taking toward your goal. When you break your large goal down, you will know what you need to be doing consistently each day, week, month, or quarter to create success toward achieving your goal.

In building my business, I have a goal with revenue targets. I have to determine how many monthly keynote speeches I need to give, how many corporate professional development trainings I need to contract to deliver, and how many corporate clients I want to coach at my current fee structure. From that, I determine how many "buyers" I need to get in front of. From there I know how many leads and prospects I need to generate, and how many referrals I need to contact. It breaks down to what I need to be doing daily to hit my yearly goal.

There may also be steps in your goal that aren't replicated consistently; they may be one-time events. What about those? Those need to be scheduled.

Do you have a planner? Either an electronic or physical planner is a must when you are breaking down a goal. You'll be getting into the *details* of what it takes to achieve your goal, and there can be a lot of them. To stay focused and not become overwhelmed, you want to schedule individual and repeated tasks to ensure they are being done. Trying to keep all of this information in your head is a recipe for stress.

CHAPTER 11

The Power of Three and What It Can Do for Your Career

"The secret of change is to focus all of your energy, not on fighting the old, but on building the new."

—SOCRATES

When your day has no breathing room, and you're feeling off-kilter because your routine has gone out the window, how do you regain focus?

Do you ever find yourself in that space where you feel you have no control? Too much to do and not enough time? Are your thoughts supportive when you're under pressure, or are you feeling self-doubt? *Can I get it all done? Will I be able to meet my goals?* Definitely not the space you want your head to be. With all that I know about creating focus and influence in business and career, this can still happen to me, but now I have a tool that helps me stay focused, and I want to share it with you.

The Power of Three

The Power of Three is concentrating your focus on three things at the beginning of each day. Now, I know you'll say there are more than three things that require your attention every day. Careers, businesses, families, friends, and other commitments require your time and attention, but I want you to pick the *top three things* you want to focus on at the start of each day when you're feeling overwhelmed and out of control.

If you're a manager, you might have a project or goals you are working on. What are the top three things you want to do today that will move you closer to that goal? Break it down to the point where you have actionable items to place in your calendar and schedule three at the beginning of each day. When you schedule them ahead of time, you know exactly where to start your workday or where to go to when the day inevitably gets off track. When you've accomplished the first three, schedule the next three.

The same thing applies to daily tasks related to your goal. Schedule them, but focus on the first three priorities each day that will give you the greatest momentum toward your goal. If you're anything like me, you'll be attracted to the easy stuff—the little items that can be accomplished quickly and then you can visibly see your to-do list being reduced. That's not necessarily the best use of your time, however.

The reason it's *three* is that three isn't overwhelming. Three is *doable*. You can wrap your head around *three*. It gives you focus. The Power of Three will give you a starting place, help you to re-establish your routines faster, and reduce your anxiety over the unknown.

Have you heard the old parable about the professor who utilizes the rocks, pebbles, sand, and water to demonstrate priorities? Here it is if you're not familiar.

There was once a professor who was giving a lecture. In front of him, he had a big glass jar. He started off by filling up the jar with large rocks, and when they reached the rim of the jar, he held it up and asked the students if the jar was full. They all agreed there was no more room to put rocks in the jar; it was full.

But was it full?

The professor then picked up a tub of small pebbles and poured these in the jar around the large rocks and shook the jar gently so that they filled the spaces around the big rocks. "Is the jar full now?" he asked. The students all looked at each other and agreed: The jar was now completely full.

But was it really full?

The professor then picked up a container with sand in it. He poured the sand over the rocks and pebbles, shook the jar gently to settle the sand, and once again held up the jar to his class and asked if it was full. Once again, the students agreed the jar was full.

"Are you sure it's full?" he asked.

He finally picked up a large bottle of water and tipped the water into the jar until it filled up all the remaining space.

The students laughed.

This story is told as a metaphor for focusing on what is important in your life, but it is also a metaphor for what you focus on in your career. The rocks are *important* things that move you toward your career goals and help you to create influence. Those are the things that you need to be focusing on *daily*. The pebbles are the other things that matter, which you need to do in your job and move you toward your goals, but not as much as the rocks do. The sand is the small stuff that can be very attractive but may not be the best use of your time if you truly want to move the needle on your career. Be careful of the water, though. These are the things that keep you busy, but not necessarily productive. These are the "time-sucks" we all can fall into, like TV, social media, water cooler conversations, and the like.

Practice the Power of Three at the end of each work day, so you know where to start the next morning. Do it on Friday, so you know what the focus will be on Monday and eliminate the Sunday-evening anxiety. Do this before you go on vacation and have a clear plan of what you'll dig into when you get back.

Thinking about and planning for the first three specific steps takes the stress off of you, even if the plan changes. You'll be giving yourself the gift of clarity on the days that you need it most.

CHAPTER 12

Achievable Outcomes: The Keys to the Kingdom

"Confidence never comes from having all the answers; it comes from being open to all the questions."

—UNKNOWN

When I speak and consult with groups, my message is always the same. Everything you *need* to do exactly what you *want* is already inside you.

Now, you may be thinking that you want to be promoted into a management role with supervisory and profit-and-loss responsibilities, and you've not done that before. You don't know how to do it, so how can that statement be true?

You may not know how to do it today, but you have the *resources* inside of you to figure it out. You can learn what you need to learn, once you have identified what it is. Remember, you can't hit a bullseye without a target.

You know people who have done what you want to do, and they can help you. There are courses you can take. There are podcasts you can listen to. There are videos you can watch. There are coaches who can assist. The list goes on and on.

When I started my business, I had never owned a business before. There was so much I didn't know, I was clearly in the space where *I didn't know what I didn't know*. But I learned. Questions are great tools, and our answers uncover vast amounts of information.

When it comes to creating a goal statement, it needs to be personal. You may get ideas from other people, but how you implement will be your own way. When you start tapping your internal wisdom, the process gets less overwhelming.

Again, make sure your goal is phrased as what you *do* want and not what you *don't*. You want to be moving toward your goal, not away from something else. If you'd like, grab a sheet of paper and a pen, follow along, and write your answers for your own personal goal.

You want to get the creative juices flowing (very important) and to start painting the full picture of how achieving the goal will impact your life. The more sensory information you can provide, the more real this goal will be to you.

- **What will achieving this goal allow you to do?** What do you get from it? Why is it important to you? Goals should be BIG. Goals should scare you a bit and certainly stretch you as a person. When you have big career goals, you need to have big motivation to help you accomplish them. I hate to tell you this, but not everything will go perfectly. You will have setbacks; you will probably have days when you want to quit. So having a thorough understanding of your goal will allow you to get clear about what your motivation is. List everything that you can think of that this goal will allow you to do, to be, to have. Is it more income? Is it more credibility? Is it a necessary step in a bigger goal of making partner or director?

- **What will you *see* when you have achieved the goal?** Example: *I see the framed Certified Financial Planner certificate hanging on my wall.*

- **What will you *hear* when you have achieved it?** Example: *I hear congratulations from family, friends, and colleagues.*

- **What will you *feel* when you have achieved it?** Example: *I feel a great sense of pride and accomplishment in myself and my efforts.* Go into as much sensory detail as you can.

- **Where are you *now* in relation to your goal?** With any goal, you have to mark a starting place so you can determine the steps it's going to take to reach it. Think of the GPS in your car. You begin from a starting point so that you can ascertain the route you need to take, the time it's going to take to get there, and even the miles you will travel. Where are you starting from?

- **If you had nothing else to do but achieve this goal, what is the *very next action* you would take?** If you don't take any action, you'll still be in the same place one year from now. To make it easier to start working toward your goal, determine the first step you would take. In the case of the CFP certification, would you talk to your boss? Acquire the exam fee? Review the CFP guide? What is the next step you would take in your goal?

- **How will you know you have achieved this goal?** When is it real for you? You always want to pick a point at which you know you have achieved what you set out to achieve. It's the finish line for the goal. If you're a Type-A, perfectionist, over-achiever, you can keep moving the bar and never acknowledge or celebrate your career victories. You'll be moving onto the next thing. Now, having a next thing is important, but celebrating what you have achieved is just as important. You're disrespecting all of your efforts if you don't. If you were pursuing the CFP, *achievement* might be when you are notified you've passed. Or maybe it's not real to you until you receive the certificate. It's when *you* know. What's your finish line?

- **Do you know anyone else who has done it?** If not, is there anyone in your network who can introduce you to someone who has? Take that person to lunch or coffee. Ask about his or her experience. Ask what guidance the person would offer after having gone through the process. People love to help other people. They love to talk about their experiences. You should be able to use that for your benefit. Shorten the learning curve a bit.

- **What resources do you already have that will help you achieve this goal?** In the case of the CFP certification, perhaps you have a solid, knowledgeable foundation, money set aside, a loan lined up, a sponsor at your company, a study group. Whatever it may be, list out everything that you can think of that works for you in getting this goal.

- **Finally, ask differently.** This is kind of a brain-twister, but do your best. What will you get when you've achieved your goal? What *won't* you get when you've achieved your goal? What will you get when you *haven't* achieved your goal? What *won't* you get when you *haven't* achieved your goal? Interesting information can come out of our brains about what specifically we want and why we want it when the questions are asked differently.

Answer as many of these questions as you can and utilize the information as your foundation for building a thorough, actionable, achievable goal. The more you can answer, the more clarity you get.

PART 3

COMMUNITY

Why You Need Community

There are a lot of logistics to creating influence in your business. To figure out what options may be available to you, how best to utilize your skill set or network, or to find and make choices that bring you happiness is a lot of information that you don't know. Otherwise, you already would have acted on it, right?

One of the most stressful things you can do is go it alone. Do you think that you have to have it all figured out? That you need to come up with all the answers? You don't. Especially when it comes to your business and professional goals, there are plenty of people who can help you along the way—if you are willing to let them.

When I was feeling stuck and frustrated in my career, I made it much worse for myself because of this reason. I was miserable to the point where I didn't recognize who I had become. I'm usually a happy person, and I couldn't come to grips with the fact I wasn't enjoying anything about my career anymore. I compounded that misery by expecting myself to "fix" what I had become by demanding that I know all the answers. When I couldn't get out of this unhappy career corner I had painted myself into, I thought there was something wrong with me, that I *couldn't* be happy in my career. I couldn't have been more wrong. I *could* find answers, just not all by myself.

When it comes to your professional life, you need to have people around you who have your back: people who get you, understand you, and support you. You need people who will tell it like it is; people who will tell you what you *need* to hear, not necessarily what you *want* to hear. You need people who lift you up, not pull you down.

You need to build a community, a tribe, a posse, a sisterhood, brotherhood: whatever you choose to call it is just fine. If you don't have something like this, you need to start building it. These are the people who are going to help you figure things out. They can share the burden, their experiences, and what worked for them or didn't. They can brainstorm with you and connect you with other people with other ideas, plans, strategies, and programs. It's a beautiful thing.

I've found that, generally, people like to help other people. If they don't care to help you or are resistant, then you haven't found the right people yet. Who are you going to let help you create more influence in your business? How are you going to go about building your community? That's the subject of our next few chapters.

What Community Is

CHAPTER 13

Strive to Thrive with Five

"You will never outperform your inner circle."
—John Wooden, Former UCLA Head Coach

W hat this quote is saying is what you might have heard already. You are the average of the top five people that you spend the most time with. Just by virtue of being together, you absorb their thinking, their attitudes, and yes, even their energy. Have you ever walked into a room and known that something was up? Ever met someone who creeped you out? Yes, you absorb and feel the energy of the people and things around you.

You Must Realize Not Everyone Is Meant to Be in Your Life

There are going to be people who don't deserve a place in your life, or at least a place in your tribe or inner circle. As a successful professional in business, you need to be surrounded by the A-Squad. If you are surrounded by those who say you're out of your mind for going after that promotion, making a move to another company, or considering a change of career, then how will you ever achieve it? Or, maybe you will achieve it, but how much harder will it be?

Here are some questions you should consider when forming (and yes, it's a choice) your inner circle. Some may not apply to your specific circumstance, or there may be other attributes you require. My point is, give it some thought and make intentional choices about who gets close to you as you are evaluating the people in and around your life.

A-Squad Clarity Questions

1. Have they been or are they now where you want to go professionally?

2. Are they supportive of you?

3. Are they willing to tell you what you need to hear instead of what you want to hear?

4. Do they encourage you to stretch professionally?

5. Will they help you brainstorm?

6. Is this a reciprocal relationship?

What do you do, though, when you discover you've got some pruning to do in your inner circle?

Here are two types of people you want to *avoid* having in your inner circle:

- The first is the *drama queen* who creates chaos. This person also generates the energy vortex you get sucked into whenever you're around them. Drama queens thrive on drama because it's all about them, and the more people attracted to that drama, the more important they feel. I used to say I was really good in chaos until I realized that was the instruction I was giving my unconscious mind, and those were exactly the kind of people I was attracting. *Lesson learned.*

- The second is the *energy vampire*, and as I've already mentioned, they suck the life out of you. These are the Negative Nellies or Nates (apologies to anyone named Nellie or Nate reading this) who couldn't recognize a positive thought if it smacked them in the forehead. They rain on everyone's parade. They are Mr., Ms., or Mrs. No. Their negativity is distracting and toxic.

What you may not realize about these kinds of people is that it takes up *your* valuable energy, effort, time, and resources just to be near them. You constantly have to shore yourself up because they are constantly pulling you down.

What can you do about drama queens and energy vampires? Well, a few things. Some are easier than others.

- **Realize it is your *choice*** to allow them to be in your inner circle. Even if you are doing nothing about these people, that is still a *choice*. Once you understand this, you have become *self-aware.* That's the first step to making any change.

- **Address the nonproductive behavior assertively.** To be a confident professional in today's work environment, you have to be able to draw the line in a respectful, yet firm way. It is up to you to take the initiative to have this conversation. It may not be an easy conversation, but you have to let them know how their negativity impacts you. You want to choose a neutral location if you can and don't couch your words or beat around the bush. Be firm and clear about what specific nonproductive behavior you are referring to, how the behavior makes you feel, as well as *changed behavior* you are asking for. Make the conversation about the behavior, not the person. Otherwise, the person may get defensive, which certainly wouldn't be productive. Remember, for you to be effective, it's important for you to be around people who are positive and supportive. *It's not your job to make sure they change.*

- **Make a conscious decision for your own well-being that you can't spend time around the person whose energy is negative anymore. And then don't.** But what do you do when it's your boss or family, and you can't just cut them out? You may have to have the assertive conversation above and create as much distance as you can, limiting your time with them to the best of your ability. You might also enlist the assistance of a buffer—someone who runs interference for you, so to speak.

Your inner circle is definitely *quality* over *quantity*.

These are relationships, just like any other type of relationship, and they require certain chemistry. Be selective about whom you let in. People love to help other people, and there is no better feeling in the world than having that circle surround you when you need it most. Notice the people you resonate with, who make you feel better, who encourage you to stretch. They'll show up when you're ready for them.

If you are reading this and know that you don't currently have this circle in your life, then make establishing one a priority. Look for opportunities to connect with others through networking (more on this in chapter 16). Ask people you know whom you might connect with for support in certain areas. You know the types of people you click with. Just make sure you're clicking with them for the right reasons and keep in mind how you can be part of a five for another's inner circle.

CHAPTER 14

Many Minds Make Light Work

"If you want to go fast, go alone. If you want to go far, go together."

—AFRICAN PROVERB

H ave you ever heard the phrase *many hands make for light work,* meaning that the more people you have helping or pitching in on a task, the faster it goes? Well, in this case, it's many *minds* make for light work, and it's the same principle. The more people or minds you have focusing on your professional goals, the more progress you can make, and what I'm referring to is mastermind groups.

In the book *Think and Grow Rich*, a "Master Mind" is said to have "The coordination of knowledge and effort of two or more people, who work toward a definite purpose, in the spirit of harmony."[3] This principle I firmly believe in, and it is one that has accelerated my career and business exponentially. It's not a new concept, since the words were penned over seventy-five years ago, but it's a good, solid strategy for anyone building, refining, or wanting to exert influence over their career.

---

[3] Hill, Napoleon. Chapter 10. In *Think and Grow Rich: The Complete Classic Text.* New York, NY: Jeremy P. Tarcher/Penguin, 2008.

A mastermind is your own *personal community* that you have selected. To build a mastermind, you find *like-minded people* who are committed to being there for you, just as you are for them. Not everyone is a good fit for the mastermind concept, especially if they aren't willing to devote time to the group. Not everyone is a good fit with each other, either. You want to start with a couple of like-minded people and then slowly expand the group.

Setting a cap on the number of people might be a good idea. You don't want too many cooks in the kitchen and the more people you have, the longer it will take to accomplish regular meetings, too. You'll also want to consider personality styles within the group; a mix works best because each style brings something different to the table. Make sure they don't conflict, however. You want to look forward to this time together.

With a group of people, you don't have to feel alone. Since you are regularly connecting, you are getting the support you need consistently. You get to share learning, and you don't reinvent the wheel and waste your time when someone has been through a similar circumstance. People have varied skills sets and something that is easy-peasy for you may just be the thing someone else in the group is struggling with, or vice-versa.

In a mastermind, you'll also be encouraged to *think bigger* because people external to us don't see the same limitations that we place upon ourselves. The idea of joining a mastermind is to stretch as a person and have the support of others in a nonjudgmental environment while you do it. If you don't reach for something outside of your comfort zone, you're doing yourself a disservice.

Mastermind Variations

- Masterminds can take place *in person*. You can physically meet somewhere at a regularly scheduled time. When I started my business, I met two other women who had their own businesses every two weeks for coffee. Their businesses weren't the same as mine, but they were entrepreneurs, and I got lots of great advice.

- They can take place *retreat-style*, going away somewhere for a determined period, like a weekend, and taking a deep dive with the group. My mastermind came down to Florida for the weekend, and we divided the time among us to devote hours to looking at each other's businesses and projects. It's also a way to connect at a deeper level with some social time built in for such activities as dinner.

I also attended a coaching mastermind retreat with a group at a conference center in upstate New York. It made such an impact because we were away from our homes and businesses for the weekend and were able to focus. We learned about the elements of speaking as part of our businesses, crafted systems to support our speaking, and then got to present and get feedback from our coach and fellow retreat members. I made huge progress in building my business that weekend. In this particular case, it was facilitated by my coach and was a paid mastermind event; it was worth every penny. The progress I made could not have been replicated in a weekly or biweekly call because it was a more comprehensive session.

- I've also experienced masterminds that have taken place *virtually* or over the phone on a regular basis. It doesn't have to cost money to host or attend; there are many free resources like FreeConferenceCall.com, Skype, or Google Hangouts. In one case, I had a mastermind (or accountability partner) who was also a member of the same coaching group as me. We met every week by phone. We'd cover our assignments from the coach to share what was going right and what we were struggling with related to the assignments. We could take an idea and build upon what the other had started with and make it better.

The Mastermind Meeting: A Sample Agenda

The mastermind meeting can be conducted in many ways, but the one that works best for me is the following:

1. Start with a celebration, something that is going right for you in your career or business. What is going right? What is one thing that went well for you since the last meeting? Celebrate it! This gets you to focus on what's going well. Too often, we

focus on what's going wrong. Starting with positivity helps you to get used to being and feeling successful when you have to actually say it out loud to another person.

2. Say what you're currently working on and/or what you need help with from the group. Be specific. What projects are you working on? What aspect of your business have you been focused on since the last meeting? Is there something you need help with? You might ask, "Is there anyone who has experience with developing a corporate policy manual," or, "Does anyone have a contact at this business?" Ask your fellow mastermind members for their wisdom. That's why they're there. Also, if they don't know, they might have a contact or suggestion regarding how you can get it.

3. Say what you need to be held accountable for. If you are going to make big strides in your business (and I know you are because you're reading this book), ask to be held accountable for a task or project. The group will then make a note and ask for your update at the following meeting. If you haven't made progress at the next meeting, it's your opportunity to share what's getting in the way of you accomplishing your goal and to get suggestions on what will help you be successful. For me, if I say to another person that I'm going to do something, then even if it's the night before, I'll make sure I've gotten it done.

Mastermind Best Practices

Make sure that everyone in the group gets equal time and support. Setting up ground rules will help. These rules might define the overall time allotted for the meeting, how much time each person has to give an update and seek feedback, and possibly the rotation of topics. Be consistent and don't let someone hijack the meeting. Make sure that you are giving the same level of support and feedback as others are giving to you.

Commitment to regular mastermind meetings from the group will be the biggest factor of success. We all get busy, and if you aren't willing to commit to the group and show up to support the others, it's not going to work. Pick a time that works for the group consistently and protect that time on your calendar at all costs.

Masterminds, like people, can come and go. Any group can be highly functioning for a period of time and then fizzle out. Your goals can change, and therefore your mastermind might change. Don't take it personally. Reach out again and start seeking a new group of like-minded people who also want to create professional influence, and start or join another.

Masterminds aren't always about the concrete things you'll get from them, like strategies and advice. They can also help you to feel more confident, not only in your goals or your business but in yourself.

Remember, what you put into it is what you will get out of it, and that can be just the clarity you were looking for.

CHAPTER 15

Networking and Mentor Mind

"Succeeding in business is about making connections."

—SIR RICHARD BRANSON

One of the most constructive uses of your time, whether you are building your business or looking to go to the next level, will be networking. People are meant to connect with people and form relationships for different purposes.

So, what do you think about networking? Do you look forward to it? Do you enjoy having the chance to meet new people and learn more about them? Or do you dread having to walk into a room of strangers (or mostly strangers) and strike up a conversation? Would you rather be doing most anything else?

No matter your thoughts on networking, it's a necessary element, and I'd like to share with you some tips that have helped me to become an expert networker and connect with amazing people. When you network correctly, you automatically get out of your own head. You're connecting with new people and learning more about them, what they do and what they're passionate about. Conversely, people get to know the same about you.

When you are networking correctly, you are sharing what you are working on now or next and creating advocates for your cause, whether that's increasing your skills, looking for a new position in your current company, changing companies, or building your business.

When I was so unhappy in my career and feeling stuck and frustrated, networking was one of the key components that got me to the next level. I knew I was capable of more in my job, but there wasn't room for growth at my company. As a matter of fact, not long after I made the decision to figure out what I wanted to be when I grew up (finally), the company announced it was being sold. I had a jump-start on what was next for me because I was already making valuable connections and by getting the word out that I was looking for something different, I found it—sort of.

Through my networking, I had come across a company that had an open position that was a perfect fit for me. I was excited and interviewed for the position with several people at the company. I walked away feeling like I had nailed it. I came to find out, however, that they offered the position to someone else. I was so disappointed. But not long after that, one of the executives from the company called and asked me to come in and see him. He said although I hadn't received the position, they felt my skills would be a great asset to their company and asked that I keep in touch. Through networking, I saw him at several other events and occasionally would email him to keep in touch. Within a year, another position became available, and they offered it to me. It was a better fit than the initial one. I was *elated*. It also came just before the doors closed at my old company—the timing couldn't have been more perfect.

This new position was one of the most pivotal positions I've ever had in my career. It helped me to understand my value and potential at a level I had never explored. It also provided neurolinguistic programming (NLP) and Huna training, which form the foundation of my business today. I literally would not be where I am today if it were not for networking.

What Networking Is and What It Isn't

Networking is simply meeting new people. It's about connecting with people and forming relationships, just like any relationship. You continue to build on these relationships. You are genuinely curious about the other people, and you want to get to know them: who they are, what they do, what their roles are and also with they're passionate about. Sure, you exchange business cards, but networking is truly about building relationships.

What relationship *isn't* is making as many connections as you can. It isn't about what other people can do for *you*, it's about what you can do for *each other*. That means you have to give the other person a chance to tell you what they're about, that you aren't the one doing all of the talking. It's not about making an ask for a job or a connection right off the bat.

It's getting to know people as people. Not as colleagues, CEOs, HR managers, or any other title. It's about people.

So, you may be thinking, *what if I am an introvert?* That doesn't mean that you can't network. It means you might do it a little more intentionally and thoughtfully. That actually might make you a better networker because you will stop to listen to the other person and really make good connections.

It's hard for some people to walk into an event by themselves and harder yet to actually introduce yourself to someone you don't know. It may be awkward or feel self-conscious. The facilitator of one networking group to which I belonged gave a great tip; she said, find someone standing off by themselves in the room. Who is the person standing in the back corner? Who is the person hiding against the wall? That person is probably just as uncomfortable as you, so you already have something in common. Go over, shake hands, and introduce yourself. It will make their day. It will also give you an easy connection and an easier way to introduce yourself to other people. Now the *two* of you can approach another person to introduce yourselves because two people doing the same task is easier than just one.

Networking Tips

Here are some things to keep in mind when you are networking and building relationships.

- **Eye contact**. Always make eye contact with the person with whom you are connecting. If you aren't making eye contact, it doesn't seem like a genuine connection, and people may wonder what you're actually about or what you may be thinking. Eye contact says you are present with them. Make eye contact, be present, and listen. An additional pet peeve is when someone is giving the illusion of listening to you, but instead, they are actually looking around the room to assess who else they can connect with. That's *rude*.

- **Shake hands.** When you shake hands, align the hands web to web (the web between the thumb and pointer finger) and match the pressure of the other person. Ladies, that means if your handshake is weak, you may need to step it up, and gentlemen, don't try to crush the other person's hand in your grip. Ease up a bit. A handshake is a crucial part of your first impression with another person. Make it count.

- **Exchange cards.** You always, always, *always* have business cards at a networking event. If you are not currently employed, it doesn't cost much to have a set printed with your basic contact information, and please don't use the kits for your home printer with perforated edges. You need something more professional than that. When you've connected with someone with whom you'd like to keep in touch, make a note on their business card.

- **Ask open-ended questions.** When you connect with someone, ask open-ended questions, meaning questions that cannot be easily answered with a simple *yes* or *no*. These questions are designed to get the other person talking so you can learn more about them and they can learn more about you. Be mindful of engaging the other person, not taking over a conversation and making it all about you. If you have trouble thinking of open-ended questions to ask, there is an acronym that will help you out. It is called *form* (F. O. R. M.). You can ask these types of questions of the people you're looking to connect with:

— *F* **stands for family.** Are they married? Do they have children? How many? Ages? Where are they originally from? This could help you establish common ground and easy topics to talk about.

- *O* **stands for occupation.** In addition to what they do for a living, you can ask what they enjoy most about their job. What is their most interesting work project? What is next for them in career or business?

- *R* **stands for recreation.** What are their hobbies and interests? What do they enjoy doing outside of work? If there's a blockbuster movie out, you can ask if they've seen it. Maybe a favorite restaurant in the area?

- *M* **stands for money.** Now, you're not going to ask a person how much money they make, but you can ask questions about things related to money, or that take money to purchase. Here are some suggestions to get you started, and I'm sure you can think of others too: You might be planning a vacation; ask what's the best vacation they've ever taken. You might be in the market for a car; ask what cars they'd consider. You might notice a piece of jewelry or a jacket they are wearing; compliment it and ask where they purchased it.

- **Ask what you can do for them.** When you're learning more about other people and building relationships, you always want to ask what it is that you can do for them. Is there someone you can introduce them to? Are they looking for clients? You may know of some or have some suggestions about who would be a good fit. Find out if there is a way that you can help. Networking and building relationships is an *exchange*.

- **Write a couple of notes.** When I get home from a networking event or other social gathering, I take my newly acquired business cards and mark down where I met the people they belong to. For instance, I'll include an abbreviation like COC for Chamber of Commerce or NSA for National Speakers Association. I'll jot down a couple of important details that I learned asking the F.O.R.M. questions. I'll make notes of important conversational highlights like hobbies, family information, and what the next step might be. Maybe you want to have lunch, or they are going to make an introduction for you, or you for them. You may think you will remember this in your head, but you won't. *Always make a note.* Better safe than sorry.

- **Connect with them on LinkedIn or Facebook.** When you get back to the office or to your house, connect with them on LinkedIn if they have a profile. When you reach out to them, write a personalized note instead of using the standard "I'd like to add you to my professional network on LinkedIn." I usually send something like this:

  > "Hello Jason, It was a pleasure to meet you at the Chamber meeting yesterday (*reminding him of where we met*), and I would enjoy staying connected here on LinkedIn. Please let me know if I can make any introductions for you (*a helpful offering*) or be of service to you or your company.

  > Be well, Debbie Peterson—Getting to Clarity." (*I include my company name since the business is different from my name*).

  Once they accept my LinkedIn request, if they are a strong contact and I would like to connect with them further, I'll send an additional message— usually something like this:

  > "Hello Jason, Thank you for 'Linking me In.'

I enjoyed our conversation at the Chamber meeting and would enjoy having the chance to speak further about it. Would you have some time for coffee or lunch in the next couple of weeks? Debbie"

In corporate business, generally, LinkedIn is the most appropriate social media channel. LinkedIn is like a big virtual networking meeting, whereas Facebook is like a family reunion. Which one you choose depends on how well you know the person and where you would be most effective at staying in touch.

If you own your own business and your main marketing which attracts your customers is done on Facebook, then definitely connect with the new contact there, and you may want to invite them to like your business page, too.

Here's an important note and another of my pet peeves: If you have an email list for your business, you *must* get permission to add anyone to it. Just because they give you their card does not give you permission to add them to your list. This is a rookie move, and there is nothing more irritating than being added to an email list when you already receive too much email. You can kill any credibility or budding business relationship by making this mistake.

You can easily get permission when you swap cards. I say something like:

"Thanks for your card. I have a newsletter that goes out once a month (*or however often you send yours*) with valuable tips, tools, and techniques for professionals to have more clarity in their career. May I add you to it? You can unsubscribe at any time."

Make sure that you stay in touch with your network. Building these relationships is not just making one connection, and then you go away forever. Networks need to be maintained to be effective. Here are some ways to stay in touch with your network:

1. Send a LinkedIn Message

2. Send an email

3. Call them

4. Invite them to lunch

5. Invite them to happy hour

6. Connect with them on Facebook

7. Send them a card

8. Make a recommendation on LinkedIn

9. Invite them to an event that will be of benefit to them

10. Make an introduction via email

11. Send a book they might enjoy

12. Email an article that will be helpful to them

I'm sure you can think of many more and others that would be appropriate for each new person you connect with. *Go for it.*

PART 4
ENGAGE

Why You Need to Engage

"All good things are just outside of your comfort zone."

—Unknown

S o, why do you need to engage? Well, by now you know specifically what you want in your career or business, or at least you have a very good idea of your direction. You've got a goal, or a plan or strategy to get you there: something that is S.M.A.R.T. You have started to develop your community, the people who support you and lift you up in creating the professional life you desire.

Where a lot of people can get hung up, though, is right here, when you are supposed to engage, take action, and be willing to move outside of your comfort zone.

Many people let the *what ifs* stop them. "What if this happens?" "What if that happens?"

You can "what if" yourself into a dead standstill. Some people will retreat to one of the earlier steps and hide behind the premise of doing "more research," convincing themselves they aren't ready yet. Some people will immerse themselves in busywork and say that they are working toward their goals, but they are *busy*, not productive. They really aren't accomplishing anything.

Have you ever walked and noticed things that were distant on the horizon? The more you walked, however, the closer those items appeared, and their true form revealed. What started out as a speck in the distance became a house the closer you got to it. Items you didn't even originally see at a distance came into view as you continued to walk forward. Taking action is the same way. If you won't start your journey and take action toward your goals, then the ideal solution for you will never become visible, because you've not made an effort to get there. It's just past the horizon, and there are steps you need to take first to have access to it.

You may be unsure or even scared. It takes a leap of faith, but it's a leap of faith in yourself. Believe me, I was scared witless when I left corporate life to start my own company. I had no idea what I was doing, but I had a really strong *why* propelling me, and I knew that I would figure it out. I let go of the limiting beliefs about myself and my abilities and knew that this was part of my destiny. Destiny: That's kind of heavy, right? But it's true; what you want is part of you as well.

I had never created a company. I had never done anything like this before. I had never been an entrepreneur. I had always worked for someone else. But because I knew the direction in which I was going, I was able to meet the people, professionals, coaches, and mastermind partners I needed to meet and do the work. I was able to learn. I was willing to make mistakes and learn from them, and believe me, I have made plenty.

I have done things wrong. I have done things backwards. I have stepped on toes. I have let things fall through the cracks. I have dropped balls, but that is not what I focus on. I have built a business doing something I love—supporting, empowering, and motivating professionals to create purpose, passion, and potential tied to performance. Each year I can look back and see the growth I've made. What a feeling.

That's what I want for you to, whether it is a corporate career or your own entrepreneurial business, I want you to continue to grow and move toward that which makes you feel fabulous.

CHAPTER 16

What It Means to Engage

"You are what you do, not what you say you'll do."

—CARL JUNG

The more you take action, the more obstacles you may encounter, and that's natural. You've got to have strategies, however, to be able to deal with things that get in your way, and I want to share some tools with you.

As part of our goal-setting process, one of the questions was, "If you had nothing else to do but achieve this goal, what is the very next action you would take?" You already have determined the first step to take. Take it. Don't think about it more. Don't tell yourself you're not ready. Don't sell yourself short. Do it. Then see what happens.

Did it work out the way you wanted it to? Kind of? If it worked out the way you wanted it to, great! You don't need to refine. It's not about perfectionism; that will only stall you. Keep taking steps forward.

The very first blog I wrote wasn't the best. I had good intentions, but I couldn't get the words out of my head the way I wanted to. I couldn't convey the right meaning in my post. If I had quit, then I wouldn't have written this book. The first blog, although not perfect, was one of the necessary steps that, when repeated, gave me the confidence to write a book. This won't be the only book, either, because taking this step will give me the confidence to continue to move forward.

But what if the action you take doesn't work out very well at all? Forget perfectionism. What if it was just a bad decision? Just as we covered in chapter 6, it's going to happen. Not everything is going to work out the way you want all of the time. If it is working out that way, odds are you're playing it too safe. When something doesn't work out the way it's planned, you still need to celebrate. You've taken action, you're not stuck, you are moving, and at this point, the mistake has been made, so it's water under the bridge. What do you want instead? How can you recalibrate so that you are looking forward again? What will you learn from this error that will allow you to take better action the next time and move you closer to your goal?

I remember having a conversation with a friend of mine over coffee. I wanted to hold a workshop to empower women professionals but was scared to do it. She had recently done one, and so I asked her for guidance. She gave me a pearl of wisdom that has stayed with me since that day. She said, "Treat it like an experiment." That was a powerful statement and took the pressure off of me to create a workshop that was perfect.

So, newly energized and still scared, I created a workshop, booked the space, and invited everyone I knew. Oh, I delivered great content, but it was dry. I mean *really* dry. None of my personality came through, and it was too much content. I was trying to "stuff" my audience because I was so concerned about providing value for my attendees. If I had quit right there, I never would have gotten any better. I got feedback from my inner circle, I determined what results I would like to be different, and then I set about making changes to my presentation to come closer to the effect I was looking for.

Today, I've been to over twenty states traveling for my business and delivered hundreds of presentations to professionals, corporations, and associations; they are fun and energizing, and my participants are engaged and have great takeaways.

One particular exercise I do with my audiences is this. I ask them spefically, what gets in the way? The answers come to me like popcorn, quick, some sweet, some salty. I often hear that it's things like time, family, spouses, fear, self-doubt, or even life that get in the way of achieving goals. It's my next question, though, that really gets them thinking.

What do you have control over? I take each answer individually and ask that question. Some barriers, people *do* have some semblance of control over, but others they don't. Still, what happens each and every time I do this exercise is that participants realize they have much *more* control than they thought they did, and that only a small portion of their perceived obstacles actually get in their way.

We have excuses, for the most part, regarding why we don't get what we want. We also have much more influence over those excuses than we realize.

If you never get out of the starting gate, then you'll never cross the finish line.

Have you ever heard the phrase, "People are their own worst enemies?" It can be true, especially when it comes to how you think while you're moving toward something new and bigger. You can engage in negative self-talk; lack focus; anxiety can come up; your mental and emotional baggage can get in the way. But what do you do when that happens? I'm glad you asked, because those are the strategies that I want to share with you next.

CHAPTER 17

That to Which You Give
Focus Expands

"Energy flows where the attention goes."

—Dr. Matt James

So what does that quote mean? Whatever you spend your time, attention, and resources on will *grow*; it will continue to increase in your life. Kind of like a magnifying glass; whatever you examine with it becomes much more *clear* and *bigger*. What you need to be disciplined about is what you *are focusing on*.

If you are thinking, "this is too hard" or "this will never work," what are you focusing on? Is it *possibility* or *impossibility*?

> By the way, I want to take just a moment here to break down the word *impossible*, because it can be looked at two ways— impossible or *I'm possible*. Same letters, big difference. Which will you choose?

If you spend much of your time binge-watching TV dramas, what are you focusing on? Is this contributing to your professional success? Is this filling your mind with new knowledge that will help you grow? Or is it an escape from frustration, anxiety, or fear?

If you are in and out of Facebook, Pinterest, Twitter, LinkedIn, and YouTube, following what other people are doing in their business on a daily basis, what are you focusing on? Their business or yours?

You've created your professional goal back in part 2 of this book, so you understand what it means to have a focus by way of a goal. You've given your mind instructions for what you seek. You've said, "This is what I want. This is what I'm expecting." Now it's time to follow through.

It's just at this time when we are ready to go for it, that our stuff comes up. We procrastinate. We get distracted. We get overwhelmed because we're not organized. I don't want that for you, so here are some things that might get in the way and what you can do about it.

You Have to Choose a Lane

Wanting it all is a huge distraction to your career and business goals.

First, let me say that I do not disagree with the idea that as a professional you can have it all. What I mean is that if you want to make meaningful change in your career or business goals, the phrase "having it all" will not help you get there. In fact, it could be the biggest obstacle to you actually achieving what you want.

About fifteen years ago, I was going through a big "I want to have it all" phase (and taking a hefty dose of "It needs to be perfect"). I felt I was responsible for everyone and everything. In my career, I wanted to be depended on, I wanted to be the go-to person, and spent a great deal of time making myself indispensable (you know there is no such thing, right?). My house needed to be perfect, my son needed to do well with grades, sports, and friends, and I needed to be the perfect hostess for my husband's business parties and dinners by cooking like Martha Stewart. At the same time, I needed to be fit, and so I headed to the gym five days a week at 5:30 a.m. and attended Weight Watchers meetings so I could fit into the clothes hanging in my closet.

I wanted it all. What did that get me? Stress. Big time.

I want something different for you.

So, I want you to consider your definition of "having it all." If you are looking to have it all in every area of your life while pursuing big goals to take you and your career to the next level, you are required to invest your time and energy across multiple areas. Your attention and focus are divided, and that is not how big change happens. To experience a big change or movement, you need to *focus*. You have to pick a lane to create influence in your career and business.

You have to be willing to put less time and attention into some areas so you can put more time and attention into your goal. If you want to make meaningful change in your career or business, that might mean you have to go back to school, take a course, or work with a coach. Maybe you need to acquire a certification, or perhaps put in long hours to earn the seat at the table you desire. If you're moving your career or business to the front burner, then something else has to be moved to the back one. It doesn't mean you still don't have a flame under the others, but it does mean that you might not give them as much attention.

Be realistic about the time it's going to take to accomplish your career and business goals. Prioritize where it's most important that you spend your time in addition to your goal. Know that you can't be *everything* to *everyone*. Even that bottle of blue window cleaner, which apparently is the solution for everything, knows that sometimes you need a *spray* and sometimes you need a *stream* to get the job done.

Now that you've picked a lane, how do you manage the lanes that need attention?

The Art of Juggling While Running

Prioritize. I don't know about you, but one of the things that can stop me in my tracks is overwhelm. Have you been there? There is so much to do that you can't even begin to speculate where to start. Everyone wants your time. All the things you said "Yes" to because none of them seemed like a big deal individually are suddenly converging at once. You wake up in the middle of the night with lists of things running through your head, and because your conscious mind is finally sleeping and out of the way, your unconscious mind is only too happy to remind you of all the things that you've forgotten. You can keep a tablet by your bed, but that's still only adding more to your plate. What do you do with it all?

You need a system to be able to recognize what is most important and the order in which you need to get it done to be the most efficient you can with your time.

Think back to chapter 13 when we covered the parable of the professor with the rocks, pebbles, sand, and water. How do you begin to put your tasks, responsibilities, and duties to work *for you*, and to work for where you are right now? Your priorities will change. The time that you can devote to your priorities will ebb and flow, depending on what is going on in your life. That's normal. If you are getting married in a month or your child needs to have surgery, your priorities will shift. You have to shift along with it because beating yourself up and stressing yourself out isn't helping you or moving toward your goals.

Do you know someone who does prioritizing or time-management really well? Is there someone in your office or life who is uber-organized? See what tips, tricks, and tools they can share that will have you racing through your to-do list in no time. You need to schedule time for what is most important because there is always something in the wings to take its place.

For me, the solution was an adaptation of several different processes that I've been taught over the years and combined into one. It is a clear, straightforward process that will help you go from frustrated to focused with your time. Here is my five-step *From Frustrated to Focused* process to help bring clarity to your day, time, and calendar.

When I've got too much going on and try to hold it all in my head, I label *everything* "Important." This process allowed me to take back control of my time, prioritize my main goals, and kick overwhelm to the curb, leaving me feeling calmer, organized, and with more clarity.

- **Step 1.** Do a brain dump. Set a timer for fifteen minutes, grab a sheet of paper and a pen, and let your brain empty out. Whatever comes to mind that you have to do, write it down. It doesn't matter if it's a professional task or a personal one (you are one person, after all); get it out of your head and onto a piece of paper. It also doesn't matter if it's something you have to do tomorrow, next week, or next year. Write it down. I like to do this first thing in the morning when the house is quiet and I've already awakened, thinking of things I need to do. No matter how big or insignificant, it all gets captured.

- **Step 2.** Now that you have a hefty list, go through each item and assign any externally driven hard due dates. If you've got to send a birthday card to Aunt Betty, schedule it on your calendar. If you have to make travel arrangements for an upcoming trip, schedule it. Make sure that you schedule it well enough in advance of when it needs to be completed. It might take a few days for you to buy Aunt Betty's birthday card, address and mail it. Allow for that time when you consider the date you put on your calendar.

- **Step 3.** Anything that doesn't have a hard due date gets prioritized. I like utilizing *A*s, *B*s, and *C*s, but you can use whatever system of prioritization that you like. For me, the *A*s are the hot items that are very important and a key to making or keeping more money in my business. Getting a contract out to a client, sending proposals or invoices, and prospecting are all *A* tasks for me. The *B* tasks are those that are important, but just not as important to those tied to business development. For me, such tasks might be working on tweaks to my keynotes or preparing a new training segment. The *C* tasks are "busy" kinds of tasks that need to be done at some point, but either aren't important or aren't important *right now*.

- **Step 4.** Anything that's left over is addressed here. If you can't easily put a due date on it, it's probably because it needs to be broken down a bit more. If one of the tasks is to prepare end-of-year reporting, you might need to chunk it down further. What are the individual elements or tasks that go into this larger task? Go down a level or two and assign hard dates and prioritize those individual tasks.

- **Step 5.** Employ the Power of Three. Once you have your scheduled and highest-priorty items identified, pick three things each day that you can complete from your *A* list within the time that you have available, *outside* of what is already schedued. You might have a day that is pretty open, and you can get something significant done like creating a new marketing piece. You might, however, have a day from Hades, and there's barely a moment to breathe. In this case, start early, before your day gets the best of you, and pick three small items from your *A* list to complete between your scheduled to-dos. This way you are always working toward your highest-priority items. If you can't complete anything from your *A* list, then move to the *B* list. Just don't get sucked into your *C* list and stay there, because that's probably just busywork, not productive work.

Here are a couple of additional tips to consider outside of the five-step process.

Delegate. If you've got a list that needs to go from *to-do* to *done*, you may need help even after prioritizing. When I'm working on something that is time-sensitive, like an article that is due for a publication, and I'm behind, I ask for help. You can do the same thing when it comes to crunch time because even though it is obvious to *you* how busy you are and that you need help, some people don't connect the dots. You have to ask for help because your family, friends, and *coworker*s aren't mind-readers.

Can someone else in your department take the meeting? If you're a manager looking to go to the next level, who are you grooming to come in behind you? You are developing yourself, but how are you developing others? Who can step in and start taking on more responsibility so that it develops them and works to free some of your time? That's a true win.

What about on the home front? Can your spouse or significant other pick up dinner? Can your kids straighten up the house? Today, with the broad use of technology you can have assistance with just about anything at home. You can ship a meal to your house, have groceries delivered, make use of the car dealership pick-up/drop off service, use a travel agent; there are personal shoppers, dog walkers, and cleaning businesses. Support your local businesses and let them support you.

As a busy professional or entrepreneur, you can wear many hats depending on the size of your business. I have three employees at Getting to Clarity. Me, myself, and I. My dog, Ernie, is in the office with me all day, so I guess I could add him as a coworker too. My point is that there are only so many hours in a day when building and running a business and you can't do it all no matter how superhuman you think you are. Can someone take on your social media posting? Manage your website? A ghostwriter for blogs? How about a virtual assistant? Have you heard of Upwork or Fiverr where freelance talent in just about any area of business can be hired to help you with specific tasks and projects?

Re-evaluate what's on the calendar. We can have a system or a routine that works for us on normal days, but sometimes when we are taking on a big professional goal or project we have to let some stuff go. If you're feeling overextended, it may be that you have a lot of items on your calendar that you said "yes" to that now need to be re-evaluated. Ask yourself the simple question, "Does this meeting, appointment, event, etc. help me move toward my goal or away from it?" You can also ask, "Is this the best use of my time to achieve the goal that I want?" When you get used to spending your time in an efficient way it will make it easier to say "No" when you need to and protect your time to make bigger progress in your goals.

CHAPTER 18

Distractions, and Sacrifices, and Shiny Objects, Oh My!

"The essence of strategy is choosing what not to do."

—Michael Porter

A s human beings, we tend to fall into routines to get things done. It's the way our minds work. The majority of what we do happens unconsciously, and usually, these behaviors are habits; that is the case whether what we are doing supports us or not.

Whenever you are reaching for something new or bigger than anything you have ever done before, it seems as if things can pop up out of nowhere to try to stop you or slow you down. It seems as if there are *never* enough hours in the day. How can one person do this? How do you have a job, a family, serve in your community, *and* do what it takes to accomplish your career goals to take you to the next level? How do you find the time to go back to school, get certified, build a business, while at the same time enjoying being with your spouse or significant other, attending your kids' activities, and finding some time for *you* when you need it most?

If you've done the work in the beginning and have clarity on exactly *what* you want and *why* you are doing it, then you'll be in a much better place. If you have your goal in mind and it's broken down into actionable steps so that you know what you are consistently doing each day, week, and month, then you are much farther ahead. If you have your inner circle created so that you are surrounded by people who lift you up spiritually, mentally, and emotionally, then you are most of the way there. But even with all of that in place, it can still be difficult to do what we most want.

Why?

We get distracted.

Has that ever happened to you?

In writing this book, some days it was difficult to find the time to do the writing I needed to do to get it done on time. Some days the writing didn't get done at all because there was so much going on, and even then, knowing that I had to get back on track, the distractions could get in the way.

What distracts *you*? What do you get sucked into that you know you shouldn't spend your time on, but just can't seem to help it? Facebook? YouTube? Text conversations? Instagram? How about TV or video games? What is getting in the way of you achieving the goal you have put so much time and effort into defining? Is the distraction worth more to you than your goal?

I want you to be successful in creating influence in your career or business, so let's discuss some strategies that help with eliminating or controlling *distractions*. What can you do? Set yourself up for success.

- **Create a successful environment.** If you are distracted by social media or other visual or auditory elements, then create a space where you won't be. Close all the tabs in your browser except those you are *working* in. Turn notifications off. Put your phone on silent, or better yet, leave your phone in another room (on silent, because you know you'll hear it and want to go answer it). Close the door. If you work at home, give the dog a bone. Do whatever it takes to make sure you create the environment to concentrate on what you need to do it without distractions. If you're in an office, you can schedule a conference room, but make sure that your boss knows where to find you. Find a coffee shop at lunchtime (I don't know why, but even though it's a public place, I can get more done in two hours there than I can in two days at home sometimes).

- **Build a new habit.** What can you do consistently to help create a new habit, which allows you to be successful in pursuing your goals? For me, it is writing first thing in the morning. I wake up, do my morning meditation, grab my coffee, and head to the office to write. I do that before I do anything else because if I say I'll get to it later, something will always come up and it doesn't happen. In addition to the book, I write for newspapers and my own blog (www.gettingtoclarity. com/blog) in the morning before the day starts because that is when I am fresh. My mind is uncluttered from the events of the day to come.

- **What if you need a break?** It can't be all work and no play, right? Sometimes you do need to just walk away for a while, and that's great unless you get sidetracked into something that is much less important. If I feel that I need a break, I pay attention to that feeling and take the time I need. I set up the break like a reward, though. So for instance, if I finish two more calls to prospective clients, *then* I can take a break. I also set up what I'm going to be doing when I come back. It may be more calls, or it may be something different (because I need to change it up), but I'm aware of my priorities and pick something that is going to continue to allow me to move forward when I return. Know where you're going to start.

Sacrifices

What you have as your next goal may be big: I mean, really BIG. And that's going to take a chunk of your time. If you are going back to school, starting a business, or pursuing a professional designation, it may take a lot of time. You will have to dedicate yourself to pursuing this goal and consistently utilizing your time to achieve it. There are going to be things that you really enjoy that you won't be able to do anymore, at least for some time. Those are the *sacrifices* that you will have to make.

Think about going on a weight donation journey. (Yes, I said *donation* instead of *loss*, because if you lose something, what do you do? You look for it, right? What can happen then? You *find* it. OK, back to my point.) If you are trying to donate weight, you have to give up some of the things that you really love for a while, right? You may have to enjoy foods in moderation. You may have to spend more time exercising. That means that chocolate cakes, soda, naps, and couch surfing marathons (which you really enjoy) have to change into something that moves you closer to your goal.

Your career and business goals are the same. To really move the needle toward what you want, to create more influence in your professional life, whether that is a career or business, is going to take time. You only have so many hours in a day, so if you increase the time invested in one area, it has to decrease in another.

When I started my business, a lot of little and bigger habits regarding how I spent my time had to change. I loved having coffee with the morning news shows, but *nothing got done* for two hours. I love fishing with my husband, or just being on the boat with him, and that has been drastically reduced. I love to entertain and cook for a table full of people; that's been modified, too. Starting and building a business takes time, and not *part*-time. I get up early and write. I have calls in the evening. I work on weekends. I travel and am away from home, but it's all worth it to me because I care deeply about what I get to do.

This is where your *why* comes in. Back in chapter 4, we discussed your *why*. So I ask you, as you get to the point where you have to make decisions, and decisions that may mean sacrifice: Will your *why* sustain you? This is the reason you have to understand, at a core level, why you want to go to the next level in your career or business, or your *why* for going after your really BIG goal. When it's personal to you, important to you, part of what makes you tick as a person, then your *why* is strong enough to sustain you through the sacrifices you will have to make.

Your sacrifices aren't just about you, though. Who else do they impact? Your spouse or significant other? Children? Friends? For me, the person most affected by my decision to start my business was my husband (and our household). My paycheck was going away for a period of time. I was spending crazy hours creating of all the little things that businesses need to have, like a website, marketing materials, and building the programs that replicated my success for others. I worked with coaches and had calls every week in the evening. Because my sacrifices involved my husband, I had a conversation to make sure he understood my *why* and was on board. I am extraordinarily blessed with a husband who supports me so fully.

You can tell if it's a sacrifice worthy of your dreams, goals, or aspirations by how you feel. If it is something you feel good about, that lights you up, that (even though it's inconvenient) you are willing to do for the sake of your goal, then you know you're on the right track. If, however, it's not pleasant, if it's dragging you down, if it constantly feels like it's a burden, then you may want to really consider why you're doing it. Your sacrifices should support you, not suck the dream or goal out of your being.

Please don't confuse that with something that is frustrating in the short term but worth it in the long term. There will be things that you don't want to do, that you don't enjoy, that frustrate you, but that need to be done to get where you want to go. I remember when I first started creating my automated emails, landing pages, and marketing campaigns. I *so* didn't get it. I just couldn't wrap my head around it, and I threw hissy fits. I was frustrated and wanted to quit a hundred times, but I didn't. I was sacrificing my time for it, but I understood why I had to do it, even though I didn't enjoy it.

So as you consider what it's going to take to get your career or business to the next level, what are you going to have to sacrifice? Is it money? Will you have to budget yourself more closely so that you can go back to school or work with a coach? Is it fewer dinners out or fewer vacations so that you can build the website or pay for the certification you need? Is it less time with friends and family because you have to study or travel? Start thinking about those sacrifices you will have to make. Are they worth it?

Shiny Objects

Have you ever walked into a jewelry store and fallen in love with a piece of jewelry that you *had* to have, only to round the corner to the next counter and find something even more captivating? Maybe you're shopping for cars, and you've got a number of them to compare on your list. Each is different, but compelling in its own way. It makes it hard to make a decision. I like to call Shiny Object Syndrome or SOS. It deserves its own category.

We can fall into this trap when we set out to do something outside of our comfort zone or something that we've never done before. Moving to the next level of our career or business is that way. If you'd already done something, you'd already be there, and what got you to where you are now is *not* what's going to get you to where you want to go next.

So how do you choose the right path?

There are many ways to get what you want next. There are several ways that you can get the experience to become a candidate for promotion. There are numerous options that you can utilize to build your business. What can happen, though, is that you see what someone else is doing and the success they are having, and you want to divert your course and do what that person is doing. You want a quick fix; you want instant success.

It doesn't work that way.

Too many diversions and you are farther behind than when you originally started. You're also probably now feeling unmotivated. You may feel like you aren't making any progress at all. You may feel like it isn't happening as fast as you'd like, and suddenly you see someone else having the version of professional success that you want; now you are tempted to divert from your race (again) and start running someone else's.

When I was starting my business, I would see other people who had exactly what I wanted. They looked so successful and were knocking it out of the park with their businesses. Facebook was full of them. Networking meetings had plenty of them. My National Speakers Association chapter meetings had one after another. If I wasn't careful, I would get sucked into their success, and it would drain any success of my own. I wouldn't be motivated any longer, and self-doubt would start rearing its ugly head.

Well, it's already being done, so why should I bother.
I'll never be able to achieve what she has.
What was I thinking to do this at my age?
And on and on.

Here's what I learned. This is *your* race, not someone else's, and you need to run it in *your* own way. I live on a marina. All kinds of boats reside and visit the marina, from 100-foot yachts all the way down to little twenty-foot fishing boats. Now you may think the 100-foot yacht with a crew and all the trimmings sounds wonderful, but that's not the case if you want to go out fishing in the bay. We have a lot of very shallow water here in Florida outside of the channels, and there is no way that the yacht could go to any of the fishing spots in the bay. It's not the yacht's *purpose* to go fishing. Its purpose is to cruise in quiet, air-conditioned luxury with all the comforts of a house, mansion, or mega-mansion— you get the point. Don't try to be a yacht if your goal is fishing.

I figured out relatively quickly that I wanted to speak to groups, conferences, associations, and businesses. That was how I would run my race. But then I would see coaches with online programs having wild success, with lots of money and clients, and I thought, *I can do that*. I would divert my attention from my race and start figuring out how I could make that happen. Then I would see someone doing crazy successful things with live workshops, and I thought, *I can do that too*, and I started figuring out how I could make that happen. Do you think if I was continually diverting from my race that I was making any progress toward the finish line? No, wasn't. All of those diversions were shiny objects that distracted my attention and kept me from making progress.

My mantra this year is *Run Your Own Race*, and I still catch myself wanting to do something that I perceive as a quick fix or more successful and I have to remind myself of the mantra. When I stick to my plan, have faith in my abilities and efforts, I make progress. There will *always* be decisions to make. When doing something new and different in your professional life, you will face decisions you don't feel prepared to make. You may feel like you don't have enough information, and you'll look to others to see how they are creating success. It's good to find ways to enhance your race; just make sure you aren't diverting from it.

CHAPTER 19

You and Your Baggage, and I'm Not Talking Suitcases

---

*"Doubt kills more dreams than
failure ever will."*

—Suzy Kassem

Have you ever felt unappreciated at work? Been passed over for a promotion? Faced position elimination as a result of a merger or acquisition? How about losing a big customer? Or financing for your start-up falling through? Have you been repeatedly told "No" when asking for the business?

Events like these in your business or career can be tough to go through. Your work is so much a part of your life that it can be closely tied to your identity—who you feel you are. I've had friends who have gone through reorganizations in the corporate world, and some have rebounded nicely and landed on their feet, and still others have not recovered. So, what's the difference? Why do some people seem to always keep moving forward while others continue the downhill slide? One of the big reasons is *emotions*.

What we *feel* affects what action we are willing to take. If something unfortunate occurs in your career or business, whether it is traumatic or just frustrating, you *feel* a certain way about it; you *feel* emotions as a result. Maybe it doesn't sit well with you; you feel upset. You dwell on it, you beat yourself up about it, and pretty soon that's all you're focusing on. It's as if you can't get away from it. You carry those emotions with you, focus on what is going wrong and how awful you feel about it, and eventually it becomes a self-fulfilling prophecy. You are pointing your mind in that direction and telling it to focus there. Let me give you an example.

You've worked long and hard in a job. There is a merger. The fallout of the merger is that your position is eliminated. You never saw it coming. You feel blindsided. Now, not only do you have to go out and find a new position, but you have to reinvent yourself because you can't find a job doing what you used to do. It's been ages since you've had to find a job and you doubt that you know how. You might feel as if doors aren't opening for you and one interview leads to another without success. You are feeling rejected. You are feeling frustrated. It weighs you down. You start thinking that you won't be able to find a job, that it will be really *hard*, and maybe even *why bother*.

You are training your mindset.

Now, emotions aren't bad to feel. They're actually good because if you didn't care, you wouldn't feel anything at all. Negative emotions come up because our unconscious is trying to communicate with us that we aren't going in the right direction—that this isn't what will move us forward. Uncomfortable emotions are a warning that we need to pursue different action.

Let's go back to caveman times, shall we? When the caveman was being chased by the tiger, his fear was the signal to *run*. Now, your business or corporate environment isn't that bad (at least I hope not), but any urgent, profound emotions we feel are meant to inspire action— and preferably *different* action, because if you do what you've always done, then you'll get what you've always got.

Sometimes, though, it's not always a traumatic event or a strong emotion around a particular circumstance that triggers action. Sometimes, it's emotions that aren't dealt with and keep accumulating. Let's say you've got a brilliant idea for a project, but your boss isn't as enthused because it's not the right timing. That's OK: You get that, and you understand. But then you get feedback on some of your work, and improvements are suggested. Next, you want to chair a committee because it's something you're passionate about and it would be great visibility for you in the company, but someone else is selected. Each of these occurrences on their own would be a blip on the radar, but cumulatively, they start to make you feel as if perhaps you don't have what it takes. All of this combined amplifies the emotions, and you start to feel them more strongly.

The problem is, when you get to this point, you are usually only focused on all of the things that have gone wrong and could potentially go wrong. Your entire focus is on the *opposite* of what you really want. You are no longer focused on your goal or outcome. You are no longer focused on what you want, what will fulfill you. Your emotions are the primary focus and are affecting your thoughts, your decisions, and the action you take, or perhaps it is inaction. Your emotions are ruling the day.

Our emotions aren't meant to be the focus for the long run. They are meant to inspire action and then fade. But here's what happens. You make them the focus, and the longer you keep carrying them around, the more you identify yourself with them and then find more of the same. It takes a lot of energy to sustain these emotions. Eventually, it requires so much energy that you can no longer sustain it. That's when you become stuck. What you feel is literally weighing you down, rendering you immobile.

The issue becomes whether you recognize the immobility or not. If you recognize where you're at and that this isn't where you want to be, that is actually a terrific first step. Nothing can change unless you recognize that you want it to change. It is said that the pain of staying the same has to outweigh the pain of making a change because change is uncomfortable for some people. That emotion, that frustration, is part of the message. It's time to do something different.

The emotions we experience let us know that we are supposed to take action. So I think back to the caveman days when he was being chased by the tiger. That fear, which is tied to our fight-or-flight response, was supposed to move him to take action and hopefully evade the tiger.

Your negative emotions around whatever circumstances you have in your career or business are there for a reason. They are telling you that something needs to change and that you need to take action. The action comes from whatever lessons we learn as a result of what we are going through.

That's the job of emotions. Once you work through the situation, get the lesson or pearl of wisdom, and make a change, you are meant to *let go* of the emotion. The transition is done. What can happen, however, is that you refuse to deal with the emotions. You don't have time for them. You're worried about how you'll be viewed if you allow your emotions to come to the surface. You want to push through and get to the other side.

That's cheating yourself.

Your mind is your biggest asset to take you to the next level of your career. If you don't heed the warnings and pay attention to what it is trying to tell you, that is a huge disservice to yourself.

Emotions at work can be a tricky area to navigate. Miscalculate, and you can be judged as not handling them well or being unable to rise to the occasion. That is why it is so important to deal with emotions below the surface, because they will keep rising to the top until you deal with them, and each time the process will be more intense so your unconscious can get your attention. I imagine the unconscious saying, "Hey, I really need you to deal with this and get your lesson so we can keep moving forward. You're holding us back by sticking your head in the sand!"

Strategies to Use When Dealing with Situational Negative Emotions

1. **Walk away.** If someone is pushing a point on you and you feel your emotions coming up, you may lash out and react. Nothing good can come of that. Tell the person that there is something you need to take care of and walk away. (By the way, there is something you need to take care of; your emotions.)

2. **Find some privacy.** Head for the restroom to ensure you have some privacy to get yourself under control. You can also take a walk outside or go to your car.

3. **Schedule a follow-up meeting.** Set up another time in the future to finish discussing the matter. This gives you a break to process why you're feeling what you're feeling so that you can come back and approach it from a more logical point of view.

4. **Make a deal.** Once you can demonstrate to your unconscious mind that you are willing to deal with your emotions and get the lesson, you can ask for a reprieve. If you're in a situation in which you find your emotions coming up, you can mentally ask yourself to get through it without excessive emotion, making the promise that you will deal with it later in the day. That's a promise to yourself, though. You have to keep it and do the work.

5. **Focus exclusively on an object in the room.** This may be enough to distract you so that you don't become teary, angry, or hurt. The caution regarding this technique is that you don't want to be seen as ignoring the person who is speaking to you; it may also distract you from the conversation.

6. **Deep belly breathing.** If you're on the phone, you can mute and take some deep belly breaths to bring yourself back to a calmer state. It slows your heart rate and can be a powerful stress-buster.

7. **Address it.** If someone insults you and you don't catch your emotions in time, you always can acknowledge your emotions and ask why the person said that. "It's apparent that what you said bothered me; can you tell me why you said that?"

The Danger of Long-term Emotions in the Body

If you keep repressing the emotions that come up, you aren't actually dealing with them. You are *accumulating* them. You continue to carry them around and become more of that person each day because that is what you are focusing on.

The danger is that *long-term* emotions are hazardous for your physical body as well. Anger, sadness, fear, guilt, and other powerful negative emotions held over long periods can lead to serious illnesses such as heart disease, stroke, digestive issues, musculoskeletal issues, reproductive issues, and can compromise your immune system and the ability to fight other systemic diseases such as cancer.

Here are some other dangers, although not physical, just as toxic to your career.

Your emotions will distort your experience of career. Whether you love your job, hate your job, want more out of your job, are having a good day or having an awful day, your entire *experience* of your professional life is created in your head. Yes, *in your head*. Your experience of career is created in your mind and then projected out from there, like a movie in a movie theater.

The good news is, you choose what gets through and affects your experience. You are the person who gets to decide if your emotions surrounding a circumstance, person, or situation will hold you back or be used as a springboard of motivation to propel you forward in your career. Accumulated negative emotional baggage related to your career is like a speck on the lens of the projector that is amplified on a screen. It lessens your enjoyment of the movie. Here's the deal though; it's your projector. It's your movie. You can't always do something about someone else, but you can always do something about yourself and what you feel.

Your emotions can also damage (or improve) professional relationships, because your emotions can be automatic, meaning you might not be aware of them (or they can seemingly come out of nowhere and suddenly affect your decision-making about other people). They can affect your unconscious biases regarding whether you think people are good or bad, talented or not, viable as a connection or a waste of time. Your emotions can cause you to label people with a broad brush of negativity. Once you label a person in a particular way, that becomes instruction to your mind: "This is what I want to find." And afterwards, every interaction will be more inclined to happen that way.

Your accumulated emotions may cause you to take things personally and feel them much more profoundly as a result. Don't get me wrong; we are meant to care because we are human beings. No one wants to feel like they aren't doing a good job or that they don't matter. If this is your focus and you are dwelling on your real or perceived shortfalls, then that is the cycle you will perpetuate unless you are willing to take action and release the emotional baggage you are carrying.

Because you're reading this book, you want to be, do, or have more in your career. You want to feel you are doing something that is more closely aligned with who you are and create the professional experience you desire. If the negative baggage you are carrying in your career is weighing you and your progress down, speak to a counselor, coach, or other professional to find the right method to deal with your emotions in the healthiest possible way for you.

CHAPTER 20

Anxiety: You've Got a Friend in Me

"What you resist, persists."

—CARL JUNG

A lmost everyone deals with work anxiety in some form or another, and anxiety usually gets a pretty bad rap.

When you feel anxious all of the time, and it becomes a daily state of being, that's when you need to rein in your anxiety. When you let anxiety rule your days, all of your focus is spent on what you don't want. Your anxiety becomes a magnet for more anxiety. It actually becomes instruction to your unconscious mind to go out and find more of the same, which is what you don't want.

Maybe you originally had a *little* anxiety which started small and related to a particular circumstance or situation but grew to the point where now it is the norm. You're worried about everything, even things you never worried about before. Being well acquainted with anxiety, I can tell you that too much of it can start to wreak havoc with your well-being—spiritually, mentally, emotionally, and yes, physically.

Anxiety becomes your constant companion, influencing your decisions and ability to perform your job well. It affects your emotional state, and your physical body, and the relationships you have, even outside of work. Like a bucket of frigid water, severe anxiety douses any joy you experience. You become your own emotional vampire—sucking the life out of yourself.

Anxiety isn't always bad, though. Anxiety can actually be leveraged for good; a "friend" in your businesses and career aspirations. But it's like that silky dark chocolate bar you love to binge on. It should only be used in moderation.

What you should know is that anxiety in life is pretty normal. It's a sign from your unconscious that you're not focusing on the right things, and when you recognize that, then anxiety becomes a tool in your tool kit, to be used for your benefit.

When you feel anxious about something at work, it may relate to something you've never tried before. It's a stretch for you, like giving a presentation in a meeting for the first time. This kind of anxiety can be helpful. It tells you that this is important to you and that you care about doing it well. This kind of anxiety will drive you to prepare, to research, to practice. That's using the emotion appropriately; it gives you the edge to do better.

Every time I go on stage, I have some anxiety beforehand. It's because I want to do well. I want to ensure that I'm delivering meaningful content to my audience that will motivate and inspire them to reach their potential in their professional lives. I continue to refine my keynotes and presentations, incorporating new content or differ-ent ways to engage my audiences, so they receive infor-mation that will change how they look at their careers and put them back in the race. Every time I do something new, I have a little anxiety, and it drives me to be better.

When anxiety isn't your friend, it shuts you down and keeps you stuck. When you give it the power to make you stop believing in yourself and your professional abilities, that's when you've got to take action. The person who is motivated, who kicks butt when it comes to goals, who is confident in his or her professional abilities is still in there. The anxiety is covering them up.

The Anxiety Reframe is the tool that I use to help turn anxiety into something more useful. Now, this is retrain-ing your mind, so it's not a one-and-done exercise. It's an exercise that needs to be used each and every time your anxiety comes up when you are pursuing your profes-sional goals. (I wish there were a magic wand to wave, but it's just not that easy.) If you practice this consistently—if you become self-aware and have the desire to experience something different—then this will work.

The Anxiety Reframe works like this. As an example, let's say you are giving a presentation at work. It's your first with the executive staff in attendance. It was doable when it was just your department, but now that the big guns are going to be sitting in, your anxiety has bumped up a couple of levels. You are worried that you'll forget your key points, that you won't be able to explain it suc-cinctly, that you'll trip over your words. You start incor-porating the *what-ifs* into the equation now. *What if my computer dies? What if the PowerPoint doesn't work?* Then you move on to what-ifs that shouldn't even be invited to this anxiety party. *What if my alarm doesn't go off? What if I get a flat tire on the way?*

You start dwelling and overthinking everything. Pretty soon, you are feeling extremely anxious. The more you think about it, the worse the anxiety gets. This feeling, though, is actually important to you, and just as we discussed before, it's meant to inspire you to a different action.

If you are focused on everything that can go wrong, is that what you really want?

If what you are focused on is an instruction to your mind ("This is what I want to find") is *that* what you want to happen?

No, it's not. This feeling is a signal from your unconscious that you are *not* focused on what you want. You've turned away from that and are focused on the opposite. Anxiety is like an engine warning light on the dash of your car. You need to take some sort of action as a result.

In this case, you need to reorient yourself to what the goal is, and here's what I want you to focus on instead.

What happens *after* the successful completion of the event? What does it look like, sound like, feel like when you make *the* presentation of your life? *After* you have totally nailed this presentation, do you see smiling faces? Nodding affirmatively? Do you hear people telling you that you are a great presenter, or that the information was very useful and helped to drive a decision? Maybe you hear someone tell you *good job*. What does it feel like to you? Do you feel accomplished? Are you feeling motivated or confident?

Create a living, breathing picture of what success looks like to you. That's the picture you go back to each and every time you start to feel anxious. You are retraining your brain to focus on what you want, and the more you practice reframing your anxiety, the feeling will eventually lessen.

CHAPTER 21

The Five Principles of Success

"Some people dream of success while others wake up and work hard at it."

—NAPOLEON HILL

N ow that you have identified your current professional goal, here is the final step to keep you moving in the right direction and achieving success after success. You've got to stay focused in your mindset, and to do that, you have to keep these five keys in mind.

1. Know what you want

At the very beginning of the book, we talked about how important it is to know what you want. You've spent some time contemplating what that is, and now have a direction to move forward in your career. You have a clearer vision of where you are heading and why, but knowing what you want is critical to more than career goals. It is instruction for your mind to focus on finding what it is that you want. Knowing what you want should also factor into every decision you make going forward in your professional life and in your personal life as well.

- **Is this time well spent?** Is what you are doing with your time moving you forward toward what you want, or is it taking you farther away? For instance, you may be considering volunteering for a committee at work. Yes, it's volunteering your time, and there is no compensation associated with it, but will it ultimately move you closer to your end goal? Perhaps it will give you much-needed exposure in the company. Will it give you access to people you normally don't have? Will it increase knowledge in an area required for your goal? Give you new skills?

  Also related to your career goal, do you know what you want out of each day? Are you building in time and making conscious choices that will incrementally move you toward the career experience you desire? How about each event you attend, book you read, or course you take? Ask yourself, "Is this the best use of my time right now? Is it ultimately moving me toward my goals?"

- **Is this money well spent?** It would be great to have unlimited sums of money to apply toward our professional goals, but usually we have to make decisions. When you know what you want and have it prioritized correctly, it is easier to make the decisions about where you spend your money and when. If you are opening a business or building your business, does it make the most sense to join a chamber? Do you need to work with a coach?

Does your marketing need to be a priority? Do you need to find someone to help you with messaging, content, or the business website?

2. Take action

You've got to be willing to take action consistent with your goal and the timeline of your goal. If you've got a big goal with a short timeline, then bigger, bolder action is required. Let's say you are a financial planner and your goal is to create a larger client base by the end of the year. It's May already. To do this, you need to add fifty more clients to your portfolio. When you consider there are only about twenty-eight weeks left in the year, and you actually have a life to live, you've got to find some ways to get in front of *large* groups of people. You've got to take bigger action.

You've got to take action consistent with your goal. If you have a goal to be promoted to the next level in your organization and all you are doing is networking or saying "Yes" to additional work being asked of you, is that specifically moving you toward your goal? It may be keeping you busy, but is it really action *consistent* with your goal of being promoted? Are you seeking out others who have similar jobs and finding out how they made it happen? Are you making yourself visible doing the work that is required of the position you seek? Have you talked to your supervisor about development goals that will move you in that direction? Have you expressed an interest in an advanced position? Have you put yourself out there?

It's easy to be busy, but what you need to be is *strategic*. When I started my business, I would rather have done anything but call prospective clients to share how I could help them achieve their business goals with their professional talent. I felt much *safer* letting them find out about me and hoping that they would call. That's not a recipe for success, and I certainly wasn't demonstrating that I had any influence in my business. If I was researching calling scripts instead of actually calling (and researching is my comfort zone), I wasn't taking action that would get me to my goal: more clients.

What are the tasks that are going to give you the biggest bang for your buck and move you toward your goal most quickly? That's what you need to be doing.

3. Pay attention

You know what you want, you're taking action consistent with that goal, and now you need to pay attention. You need to be aware of how the action you are taking is working for you. You plot a course toward your goal, but you have to be observant enough to know when something isn't working, or the course to your goal needs to change.

There are many ways to reach a goal. The example I use in my workshops is how to become a millionaire. What are all the ways you can become a millionaire? I get answers like:

- You can work hard and earn a million dollars or more.

- You can build a business and sell it for a million dollars or more.

- You can come from a family that is wealthy.

- You can be adopted by a family that is wealthy.

- You can marry into the money.

- You can win the lottery.

- You can also be a billionaire and make some *really* bad decisions.

My point is, with any goal, you've got options. Things change as you take action and more or different options come along to help you move more quickly toward your goal. But you have to be aware and recognize when that happens. The most successful people are always looking for opportunities.

People can come into your life who are influencers in the area of your goal. By connecting with them, you can find shortcuts to progress. Maybe they can mentor you or introduce you to others who will fast-track you to your goal. They may know of companies looking for an individual like you. They may be aware of just the business opportunities you are seeking.

There may be a coach who can help you develop the skills and confidence necessary to move more quickly toward your goal. When I started my business, I made an investment and worked with a coach who cut the learning curve of creating a business as a speaker. The knowledge she passed onto me and that I paid for would have taken me *years* to figure out on my own. It was worth every penny.

A management training program might become available that isn't widely advertised within your company, but you happen to overhear someone mention it, so you inquire about it and are eligible. It might just seem like you were in the right place at the right time (and yes, that could be the case) but if you weren't paying attention, you likely would not have heard the conversation. Now you've got a shortcut to where you want to go and have increased visibility within your organization by being in the program.

Things like that happen when you are paying attention and have the right mindset, open to the feedback you'll get as you take action. Watch *The Monkey Business Illusion* on YouTube.[4] It's a perfect example of what I am speaking about. You look for and find what you give your mind instruction to seek, but sometimes it's at the expense of something that could really help you. Have a goal and a plan to get there, but be willing to see other options and explore their validity.

4. Be flexible

Being flexible goes hand-in-hand with paying attention. As you are taking action toward your career goals and you are getting feedback on your progress, you've got to be willing to take different action with that informa-

---

[4] https://www.youtube.com/watch?v=IGQmdoK_ZfY

tion. You've got to be willing to be flexible with *how* you achieve your goal.

Your end goal, whatever you want in your career, is *what* you are working toward right now. *How* it happens is where the flexibility comes in. You have a plan, but you need to be open and flexible with how your plan is implemented.

Say you are in sales in your company and you have a goal to become a regional sales manager with a salary target that will allow you to live much more comfortably. It's the natural next level in your career. You become aware through a colleague, however, of another position that is coming open for a product marketing manager. It's intriguing to you, utilizes many of your skills, the salary is close to your goal, and you won't have to live out of a suitcase. It also allows you more opportunities to progress within your company. Are you flexible enough to pursue the new opportunity?

When I created Getting to Clarity, the company was geared toward empowering women. What happened, though, was I started getting pushback from men. They wanted clarity, too. I started hearing from my marketing team that my message was applicable to both genders and that I was leaving half of my potential customers on the table. I embraced flexibility and tweaked the brand with that feedback in mind.

5.Be excellent

Be excellent no matter what you do.

If you are the entry-level auditor in an accounting firm and you are a "road warrior" because you travel so much, be excellent. It may not be what you ultimately want to do, but it's a necessary step to get there.

Excellence is a mindset. It is a habit that you can create and it starts when you are doing the things you *don't want to do*. Do them to the best of your ability. Keep learning how to do them better at whatever level you are at.

Learn from those who are doing it better than you. Model them and become even more excellent at what you do. Excellence is a moving target. If you are not improving, then you are declining, because even if you have plateaued, others are continuing to improve.

Start wherever you are and learn how you can do better. I cringe when I think of some of my earlier speeches, and I'm sure a few years down the road, I'll think the same thing about where I am today. I continue to learn about my area of expertise and new ways of how I can deliver crucial information to professionals so that they can achieve more results. I am always looking for ways to become more excellent in my craft.

If you are volunteered to be on a committee—be excellent. If you got the dreaded holiday shift—be excellent. If you're in the mail room but aspire to be in management—be excellent. When you learn to be excellent early on, and you build that habit, it makes it easier to be excellent later on, when the impact on your career is much greater.

Think about it now: What are three ways in which you can up your excellence game *right now*? What are three steps that you can take or habits that you can create to become more excellent and move you toward your career goals? Write them down. Commit to taking action right now.

1. _____

2. _____

3. _____

And in Closing

"In the gap between dreaming your dreams and living them, is the action it takes to make them come true."

—Unknown

I hope this guide helps you to move forward toward your professional goals. When I learned what I've shared with you here, my life changed, which is what compelled me to write this book. Here are some final thoughts as you move forward.

- **Be gentle with yourself.** There is no greater foe to our professional goals and dreams than ourselves. This is a process, and it will take time to create healthy new professional habits. It took time for you to learn what got you stuck in the first place. Undoing that will take time as well. Practice makes permanent.

- **Be curious.** When you find yourself in a space where you feel overwhelmed or stuck professionally, cultivate curiosity about what you want instead. That will reposition you for forward momentum.

- **Be grateful.** Celebrate all wins, no matter how large or small. Be attuned to what goes right as you move forward professionally, especially when you find yourself dwelling on everything you think is going wrong.

If I can be of good service to you or your organization as a keynote speaker, corporate trainer or coach, I'll be delighted to connect.

Debbie@GettingToClarity.com
www.GettingToClarity.com

Here's wishing you the clarity you deserve.

About the Author

Debbie Peterson was born and raised in Erie, Pennsylvania and enjoyed several corporate positions in her career until one day, instead of feeling successful, she felt stuck, stressed-out, and incredibly frustrated. Knowing that something had to change, Debbie started getting clarity and uncovered the personal process that would lead her to abundant professional satisfaction and success on her terms.

Debbie Peterson is an author, keynote speaker, corporate trainer, and mindset strategy coach who works with professionals to develop a winning personal mindset so they can accelerate their professional results. Debbie's research and experiences have shown her the power of thoughts and the ability to harness thoughts to create an amazing career and life.

As a result of her work, clients often share they have more focused control of their day, more certainty in making decisions, and more momentum for meaningful results.

Debbie is the founder and president of Getting to Clarity, LLC, a professional consulting and coaching firm, a professional member of the National Speakers Association, and a Certified Trainer of NLP (Neuro-Linguistic Programming) through the Association for Integrative Psychology (AIP). She is also a student of Huna, a modern label for an ancient system of empowerment and flexibility of the mind, body, and spirit.

Debbie also serves on the board of ATHENA International, an organization with a mission to honoring, developing, and supporting women leaders from the classroom to the boardroom.

On a personal note, she chases sunshine every winter from Pennsylvania to Florida with the two loves of her life: her husband, Tom, and a beagle named Ernie.

You can find more at www.GettingToClarity.com.

Resources

Want More? Nothing worth anything is a one-and-done. It takes continuous movement towards your goals to achieve them, but that doesen't mean it has to be difficult. With more clarity, you can be more confident, not only in yourself but in your direction of career. Clarity allows you to be more self-assured and make better decisions with less stress. It gives you the freedom to explore your purpose, passion, and potential, and actually achieve it.

If access to more clarity is what you're looking for, then I want to give it to you. I've created the G2C (Getting2Clarity) Trunk Show, which has all my resources in one place to help you continue to move forward and achieve next level growth in your career.

Visit https://gettingtoclarity.com/speaking/the-trunk-show/ for resources like:

- Checklists for networking, mentoring, and more

- Productivity tools

- Webinar replays

- Video tips

- Recommended reading and more.

Works Referenced

Bariso, Justin. "It Took Sheryl Sandberg Exactly 2 Sentences to Give the Best Career Advice You'll Hear Today." Inc.com. October 31, 2016. https://www.inc.com/justin-bariso/it-took-sheryl-sandberg-exactly-2-sentences-to-give-the-best-career-advice-youll.html.

Hill, Napoleon. Chapter 10. In *Think and Grow Rich: The Complete Classic Text*. New York, NY: Jeremy P. Tarcher/Penguin, 2008.

Simons, Daniel. "The Monkey Business Illusion." YouTube. April 28, 2010. https://www.youtube.com/watch?v=IGQmdoK_ZfY.

Szegedy-Maszak, Marianne. "Mysteries of the Mind Your Unconscious Is Making Your Everyday Decisions." *US News & World Report*. Last modified February 28, 2005. https://web.archive.org/web/20050224091139/http://www.usnews.com/usnews/health/articles/050228/28think.htm.

57024926R00102

Made in the USA
Middletown, DE
27 July 2019